A Woman's Call to Prayer

Elizabeth George

HARVEST HOUSE PUBLISHERS

EUGENE, OREGON

Unless otherwise indicated, chapter opening quotes are taken from Elizabeth George, *A Woman After God's Own Heart* (1997), *A Woman's Walk with God* (2000), and *Loving God with All Your Mind* (1994), published by Harvest House Publishers, Eugene, Oregon. Used by permission.

Every effort has been made to give proper credit for all stories, poems, and quotations. If for any reason proper credit has not been given, please notify the author or publisher and proper notation will be given on future printing.

Cover by Terry Dugan Design, Minneapolis, Minnesota

Cover photo © Victoria Pearson/Botanica/Getty Images

Acknowledgment

As always, thank you to my dear husband, Jim George, M.Div., Th.M., for your able assistance, guidance, suggestions, and loving encouragement on this project.

Contents

Discovering God's Formula for Effective Prayer

Developing the Habit of Prayer

An Invitation to... Become a Woman of Prayer

*I*f you are like most women (and like me!), you can always use a little helpful motivation for improving and refreshing your commitment to pray. That's why I've written this practical book—to help you make your desire to pray a reality.

In this written-from-the-heart book, I share my personal discovery of the blessings of prayer and the prayer-journey I began some 20 years ago. As you read, you'll find out—first and foremost—what God says about prayer! You'll also enjoy stories from the hearts and lives of Bible characters. And almost every page brings you inspiration and instruction from men and women who have answered God's call to pray down through the centuries.

To share what I've learned as a busy woman about making time to pray, I've included...

...*24 Practical Ways to Become a Woman of Prayer*—You'll discover what to do...and what not to do. And you'll understand why you don't do what you want to do—pray—and why you do what you don't want to do—neglect your prayer-life!

...*Checklists for Prayer*—Each chapter concludes with three immediate steps you can take—today!—to help you make your dream of becoming a woman of great prayer a reality.

...*A Prayer Calendar*—I've included a reproducible "Prayer Calendar" at the back of this book. Be sure you make a photocopy before you use it or mark on it. You'll want to use it year after year as you journey deeper into a life of prayer.

I've also written a companion volume—*A Woman's Call to Prayer Growth and Study Guide*—just for you. This companion volume will further ignite your desire to make prayer a reality in your life. As you work through the practical insights, scriptures, and helpful hints included in this wonderful growth guide, you'll find yourself answering God's call to prayer.

Dear friend, whether you are a seasoned prayer-warrior who aspires to continue in the battle, or a prayer "wanna-be" who wonders how to take that first proverbial step toward communing with "the Eternal," this book is for you. No matter whether you are single or married, young or old, a seasoned saint and pray-er or a newborn babe-in-Christ, you'll benefit from God's timeless guidelines for prayer.

So journey on! And share your journey with others. With this book in hand, you can...

...read it alone to enhance your personal prayer-life,
...read it along with a friend or small reading group,
...read it in a women's Bible study,
...read it in your women's Sunday school class,
...of course, share it with others.

Every woman who loves the Lord desires to pray. Prayer is the "highest activity of which the human spirit is capable."[1] Through prayer you...

...worship God,
...honor the character of God,
...bring your necessities before Him, and
...enter fully into one of the privileges you have as His child—that of communing with the God of the universe.

Beloved, if all of this is true, why wouldn't you pray?!

It's fun to talk about prayer
and easy to think about prayer.
But to actually put your feet—and heart!—
on the pathway to prayer,
to make your desire to pray a reality,
requires discipline.

—ELIZABETH GEORGE

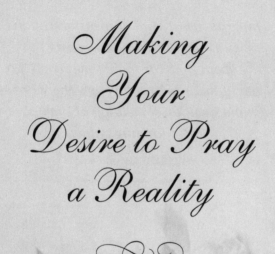

*Making
Your
Desire to Pray
a Reality*

*Imagine what kind of transformation
would occur in our hearts
if we spent time (or more time) each day
drawing near to God through His Word—
time spent on something of eternal,
life-changing value!*

—ELIZABETH GEORGE

Beginning the Journey into Prayer

Prayer.

Just say the word and I begin to yearn and squirm at the same time! As a woman after God's own heart, I *yearn* to pray. My soul longs for it. My spirit craves the communion with my heavenly Father that only the act of prayer provides. My heart emotes along with the words of King David of the Old Testament, "As the deer pants for the water brooks, so *pants* my soul for You, O God....My soul *thirsts* for You; my flesh *longs* for You" (Psalm 42:1; 63:1).

And yet I also *squirm* at the thought of prayer. Why? Because even though I know praying to God will most definitely be rewarding and a blessing, I also know it is a serious undertaking. Approaching our thrice-holy God, while both a joy and a privilege, is an awesome and almost fearful consideration. Then there is the challenge of finding and making the time, of seeking out and arranging for solitude, and of putting forth the effort focused communion with God through prayer requires. What a battle! I fully recognize that I need to pray. Furthermore, I want to pray. I covet the desired results and blessings reaped through prayer. And yet there is the sober recognition of the work and the discipline such communion calls for.

Do you, dear reader, share these same mixed sensations? Then together let's purpose to heed God's call to us to be women of prayer...no matter what! Let's embark on a joint journey of learning more about prayer. Let's seek a life lived "on bended knee."

Hearing God's Call to Prayer

Ultimately a first beginning step must be taken to launch out on any journey because, as the well-known saying goes, "Every journey begins with a single step." And that's true, too, of a journey into prayer. Even today I still remember the first step that I took toward seriously learning to pray on bended knee...

Little did I realize on Mother's Day, May 8, 1983, that God was setting into motion His invitation to me to begin my own personal journey into the depths and disciplines— and delights!—of becoming a woman of prayer. On that particular Mother's Day, my daughter Katherine gave me the gift of a little blank book, a tiny wordless book. It was purple...and I still have it.

Needless to say, that tiny purple wordless book is still a real keepsake to me for numerous reasons. But the main one is that Katherine gave it to me. She had initiated and arranged with Jim (my husband and Kath's dad) to do extra work chores to earn the money to purchase a Mother's Day gift for me. Then the two of them had gone off together to shop for just the right present for Mom. The little treasure was then painstakingly inscribed by Katherine on the book-plate in her juvenile printing, lovingly gift wrapped, and proudly presented to me on that Sunday morning those many years (actually two decades!) ago.

Oh, believe me, I screamed! I squealed! I did everything but turn cartwheels to express my thankfulness to my sweet daughter. But then I faced a problem. I don't know about you, but I never know what to do with a wordless book. I mean, they are just so…blank! Their covers are breathtaking works of art, but inside they are just so…blank! So what to do? For a number of months I let the tiny purple wordless book lie on the coffee table and began to faithfully dust around it each week. I wanted my dear Katherine to know how much I truly appreciated it.

Then one day in a dusting frenzy, I moved the tiny purple wordless book over to the edge of a shelf in the bookcase and began to religiously dust around it there. And then the fateful day came when, in yet another dusting frenzy, I slipped the lovely tiny purple wordless book in between two other books in the bookcase…and it was gone forever. Until September 12, 1983, four months later, which was my tenth birthday in the Lord. I was sitting at the old farm table that served as my desk and the place where I had my daily quiet time. As I sat there, I looked backward over my first ten years of being a Christian. Soon I was profusely thanking God for His mercy, His grace, His care, His guid-ance, His wisdom, my salvation through Christ….

On and on my prayers of thanksgiving to God gushed. Then after dabbing my eyes and nose with a tissue, I turned my thoughts forward and I earnestly prayed to the Lord, "Lord, as I embark on a new decade of walking with You, is there anything missing from my Christian life that I should concentrate on for the next ten years?"

Dear friend, I can only report to you that before I put the question mark on the question, I knew in my heart what the answer was. It was *prayer!* And suddenly I knew I had "heard" God's call to prayer. And just as suddenly, I knew what to do with that tiny purple wordless book. I ran to the bookcase, pulled it out, opened it up, and wrote on the very first page: "I dedicate and purpose to spend the next ten years in the Lord, Lord willing, developing a meaningful prayer life."

Making a Commitment

Why did I choose ten years when making my commitment to answer God's call to prayer? Perhaps it was because it was my tenth spiritual birthday. Without having written it out formally, my first decade as a Christian had been devoted to reading, studying, and getting acquainted with the Bible.

Or...perhaps it was because of my special friend Pat. Pat was a Christian mentor to me who constantly told me that I should never undertake anything that I was not willing to devote ten years to developing. And precious Pat's case for making long-range commitments has certainly proved true in my life. For instance, I've taken tennis lessons five or six times in my life. And I've taken golf lessons three or four times. But because I didn't make a serious commitment to either, it was easy to give up on those endeavors. To this day, I still cannot play tennis or golf very well! The same principle would be true of any venture...such as learning to play the piano, to speak another language, to become an artist, or...to become a woman of prayer!

For whatever the reason, I picked ten years for my commitment to develop a meaningful prayer life. And I want to testify to you right now—I am *still* learning how to pray! We just don't arrive one day at the point where we can mark "learn to pray" off our to-do list! It's as my Jim always says, "If you want to humble the mightiest Christians, ask them about their prayer life." No, none of us prays enough. None of us prays as fervently as we would like to pray or should pray. None of us prays for as many people as need to be prayed for.

And so it is an ongoing challenge to continue in the journey of prayer until we "get it," until we can even say that we've begun to know something about prayer and a little bit about how it's accomplished. And until that happens, a lot of us pray what I call "Christopher Robin" prayers. He's the little boy who struggled with his evening "Vespers."[1] He became so distracted by anything and everything that he couldn't remember who or what to pray for. He ultimately ended up praying "God bless_____" prayers, filling in the blank with each of his family members' names.

Can I ever relate to Christopher Robin's "prayer" experience (and maybe you can, too)! That's exactly how I prayed…that is, before my commitment to answer God's call on a Christian's life to pray. Yes, that's how I had prayed. And, like little Christopher, my mind wandered. I didn't know who to pray for or how to pray for them. So my prayers basically consisted of a few stabs and weak efforts, until they wound down to a muttered "God bless me and my family today."

But, praise God, I can say that some progress has been made! I believe my prayers and my prayer-life have matured. And I want to quickly say, no, I have not yet arrived. Being a woman of prayer is still a daily challenge and constant struggle. And I suspect that it will always be that way until I see my Savior face-to-face.

In the chapters to come, we'll go deeper into what it means to answer God's call to prayer. But for now (and at the end of each chapter) I want us to pause and consider the practical steps we can take *right now* to grow in this most vital area of every woman's life and in her heart-relationship with God.

Checklist for Prayer

✓ *Pray now!*—It's one thing to read about prayer, to talk about prayer, to dream about being a woman of prayer. It's quite another thing to actually pray! So Step 1 is this: Put your book down, grab your kitchen timer, and go somewhere where you can shut the door or be alone. Then pray for five minutes. Use these initial golden minutes to share with your heavenly Father your heart's desire to answer His call upon your life to become—and be!—a woman of prayer.

✓ *Get organized*—Round up some kind of notebook. It can be a spiral stenographer's pad, a yellow legal pad, a three-ring binder, a section in your daily planner, a leather-bound journal. Whatever it is, do what you can to make your choice personal, pleasing, and inspiring. For instance, is your favorite color purple? Then find, purchase, or create a purple prayer notebook. (And don't forget to include a pen with purple ink!) Don't worry about your choice being permanent. And don't get hung up on needing to make the "right" choice. Just choose something that will aid you and inspire you to take your first beginning steps down the path of your journey into prayer.

I just looked in my own little purple wordless book, and my last entry in it was 11/22/83...which means it served me well for ten weeks...which means it was enough to strongly launch my commitment to learn to pray...which also means it was enough to reveal my need for a different kind of record-keeping tool. This is probably what will happen to you as you hone your prayer skills and mature in your prayer efforts. You'll be growing as your journey into prayer lengthens.

✓ *Look ahead*—Look over...and pray over...the next week on your calendar of events. Pay particular attention to the pattern of your life—of your daily routine, of the needs of those in your family or those closest to you. Then mark on each day for the next week the exact time you will designate as your prayer time. It can be the same time each day, or it can be tailor-made to fit the demands and schedule of each individual day. Next mark your prayer appointments in ink on your calendar. Then be sure you keep them...just like you keep your dental, medical, beauty, and lunch appointments. As one of my principles for prayer states, "There is no right or wrong way to pray... except not to pray!"

For an ongoing record of the fruit of your commitment to pray faithfully, I've provided a "Prayer

Calendar" in the back of this book. Just shade in the squares for the days you do pray, and leave those blank when you don't pray. And then, my dear friend, one picture is worth a thousand words! One picture tells the whole tale. Now, what tale will your efforts in prayer tell?

Answering God's Call to You

Prayer is truly the queen of all of the habits we could aspire to as women of faith. I know we've addressed the seriousness of prayer. And we've noted the discipline and diligence a life of prayer requires. But as we leave this chapter about "Beginning Steps in Prayer," I want you to take yet another thought with you.

> He who has learned how to pray
> has learned the greatest secret
> of a holy and a happy life.[2]

I'm sure you caught the word "learned." But I hope and pray you also caught the pay-off to all of your learning and all of your efforts and perseverance in prayer—"a holy and a happy life"! And the beautiful miracle is that a holy and a happy life can be yours each day, one day at a time, as you answer God's call to pray on a daily basis. So let the outpourings of your heart begin now—*today!* The opportunity and privilege of talking to God through prayer is yours...*if* that is the desire of your heart and *if* you act on that desire. Now, what will your beginning steps be?

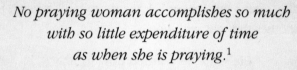

No praying woman accomplishes so much
with so little expenditure of time
as when she is praying.[1]

—C.E. COWMAN

Ten Reasons Women Don't Pray–Part 1

hy is it that so many of the things we as responsible women must tend to in life are hard to do...or at least hard to make ourselves get started on? For instance, getting out of bed in the morning. For me, this is one of those hard-to-do things (and I'm sure you agree!). Taking care of daily housework is another. And my list continues—starting the evening dinner, cleaning up after meals, washing and folding laundry, climbing onto the treadmill, maintaining a rose or vegetable garden, watering the lawn, pulling out the needed items for that all-important project, calling to make overdue doctor and dental appointments. On and on the list of a busy woman's "musts" and "have-to's" goes, a list of vital and important things to complete that are necessary, needful, non-optional—and that others depend on us to do.

But then there is "The Most Vital and Important 'Thing'" we as God's women "must" get around to and "have to" include in our every day, and that is *prayer*. And I'm sure you've found that no matter how difficult it is to work at menial chores and physical household maintenance and professional career duties, it is even harder when it comes to the mysterious, invisible, celestial *spiritual* discipline of prayer! And if a woman isn't careful, she will spend all day and all night doing the easier tasks, the less-important tasks, the secondary tasks, the trivial tasks, even the unneeded tasks—anything!—to put off the most-difficult-yet-most-rewarding "task" of all—praying!

Exactly why is it so hard for us to pray? As we've already agreed, we want to pray. And we certainly know that we ought to pray and that we need to pray. Plus there is not a doubt in our minds that prayer is critical to every facet of our lives. So why is it so hard for us to pray? As I thought through the Scriptures and looked at my own heart and life, a partial list of reasons—and excuses!—emerged.

1. *Worldliness*—We live "in the world" (John 17:11) and are affected by our worldly surroundings more than we realize or think. There is nothing in the world that encourages us to pray. Instead we are bombarded by "all that is in the world—the lust of the flesh, the lust of the eyes, and the pride of life," all of which is "not of the Father but is of the world" (1 John 2:16). There are no voices in the world admonishing us to be spiritually minded. And prayer is a *spiritual* exercise.

But prayer and praying give us a measure of immunity against the world. For instance, I've noticed that when I get up early and make prayer a priority and take the time to seek God through His Word and prayer, a fire of passion *for Him* is ignited, fueled, and fanned until its flame is brilliant and fiery. My time spent answering God's call to prayer causes everything to point upward. My thoughts, my heart, my concerns, my focus, my desires all become more noble when time is taken to lift my heart heavenward through prayer. And like an eagle that has taken flight, there's no coming down until the day is done. My soul, efforts, thoughts, and work for the day soar high above this world. They become *other*-worldly!

And then a curious thing happens. I look on my "to-do" list at the errands I originally thought that I absolutely *had* to run, the things I believed I absolutely *needed* to purchase, the projects I imagined I simply *must* undertake, the way I thought I—earlier, before prayer—desired to spend my time, money, and energy for the day...and suddenly I don't want or want to do any of them! And my loss of interest is not because of laziness or tiredness. No, it's because my previous pre-prayer desires simply lost their appeal. Their importance and excitement fades until...well, I just care nothing about them! I did what I *had* to do and *needed* to do—*pray*—and afterward everything changes because my soul is satisfied.

As the psalmist declared of God, "*He* satisfies the longing soul, and fills the hungry soul with goodness" (Psalm 107:9).

And as the hymn-writer expressed it, when you "turn your eyes upon Jesus...the things of earth will grow strangely dim in the light of His glory and grace."[2]

So watch out for the world! Resist the hold of the world on your heart by watching in prayer (Matthew 26:41).

2. *Busyness*—Another reason we don't pray is because we don't take the time to pray. And usually the culprit is busyness. And don't get me wrong! All Christian women are busy, and they should be. The Bible clearly instructs that a

strong work ethic is godly, wise, and a mark of a woman of strong character. So what can we busy women do about the reality of our busyness and the tension it places on our need and desire to be women who pray?

The story in the Bible of the two sisters who hosted Jesus and His disciples in their home shows us that a priority-order must be established between our *spiritual* duties and our *daily* duties and then carefully guarded. The tale of these two sisters teaches us that there is a need in every woman's life to acknowledge the priority-order between these two types of duties every day. The women's names were Martha and Mary, and you can read about them in Luke 10:38-42.

In a nutshell, Martha, the older sister, was a woman characterized by busyness. Hers was a life consumed with service—with puttering and fluttering, with stewing and doing, with compulsive attention to details, all carried to such a point that she "lost it" on the glorious day when Jesus came to stay a while at her house. She literally fell apart when her sister stopped her kitchen work to go sit at the feet of Jesus, God-in-flesh!

Clearly both sisters loved Jesus. And it's obvious that both served Him. But Mary, as Jesus pointed out, knew when to stop with the busyness and do the best thing, the *one thing* (verse 42) that is most needful, necessary, and meaningful—to spend time with God.

And, dear sister, you and I must do the same. We must learn to stop in the midst of all of the busyness and to stop *all* of the busyness...and pray. A woman who is too busy to pray is simply too busy!

3. *Foolishness*—Whenever we become consumed with what is foolish and trivial, we will also surely find ourselves

failing to pray. It's a given! (And I'm sure we would both agree that failing to pray might well be the ultimate act of foolishness for a woman of God!) And then our devotion to what is shallow further ingrains itself as, due to neglecting our prayer life, we become even more engrossed in and devoted to secondary things until we lose our ability to know the difference. Soon we can no longer discern between good and evil (Hebrews 5:14), between what is wise and foolish, between what is essential and meaningless.

And then what happens? We lose sight of *the* primary thing in life—our relationship with God. We foolishly and frivolously begin to spend our very limited and priceless time and our already-insufficient energy on wrong and inferior things. We fail to "seek first the kingdom of God and His righteousness" so that all the other things we need in life can be added to us (Matthew 6:33).

But praise God, the opposite is true when we pray! God gives us wisdom, *His* wisdom! *He* helps us to wisely discern and tend to our true priorities. *He* directs our energy, efforts, and time toward that which truly matters in the big picture of life—the kingdom of God and "kingdom living"—living our life as God means for it to be lived.

As the voice of martyred missionary Jim Elliot admonishes us, "He is no fool who gives what he cannot keep to gain what he cannot lose." That's the way it is with secondary things—comfort, security, money, fashion. They are "not of the Father but [are] of the world" and will most definitely "pass away" (1 John 2:16-17). They will be lost.

So pray, dear one! Commit your life to what counts, to what *really* counts. Focus your life on the greater rather than the lesser, on the eternal rather than the earthly. That's what the wise woman does, and it's done through prayer.

Checklist for Prayer

✓ *Evaluate your heart*—Identify three things you can do to turn your back on the world and your heart toward spiritual things, toward the heavenly, toward the eternal. I know that as a young Christian, who was also a young wife and mother, I had to turn my back on some of the most popular women's magazines. The more I read my Bible, the more I realized those periodicals were feeding me a steady diet of worldliness. Sure there was some practical help there. But overall, the messages being delivered were the exact opposite of the messages God's Word was sending to my heart. So check your daily input. And check your environment. What...or who...is influencing you? And is it influencing you positively for the things of God?

Now, how can you "turn your eyes upon Jesus" so that the things of this world will grow steadily more dim?

✓ *Evaluate your lifestyle*—Think about your daily routine and note the multitude of ways you spend your God-given time (some of which is meant to be spent in prayer!). When I first decided I wanted to make or find time for prayer, I discovered some truly amazing ways I was spending my time! Ways like running errands every day...just to get out of the house. Like taking a break by plopping down on the couch, turning on the TV, and flicking through the channels until I found something that interested me. Like gabbing—and gossiping!—with friends on the phone.

It became very obvious that I had plenty of time for peripheral activities and pursuits, but no time for prayer. Finally, after much prayer (and a great deal of ruthlessness!), I got things turned around until prayer came first. Then, once again, the lesser things strangely lost their appeal. They faded in importance in the light of the greater joy and satisfaction of praying.

Now, how can you make time for "the one thing" that Jesus pronounced most needful, for "the one thing" that shall never be taken away from you? How can you make time for prayer? How can you make your desire to pray become reality?

✓ *Evaluate your priorities*—Ask God to show you areas of foolishness in your life. (I know, we hate to admit it, but it's true—they're there!) Pray this prayer: "Lord, please reveal those things in my life that are secondary to a life committed to prayer. What lesser things are wasting my time and energy? What foolish things are wasting my time and energy?"

Now, as God is faithful to show you these unwise things or practices, don't foolishly neglect to follow through and rid yourself of them. We are not only to identify and confess those things that keep us from being women of prayer—but we are also to forsake and put them away (Proverbs 28:13).

Answering God's Call to You

Pardon me for speaking to your heart by using military terms. But my Jim served as an Army Reservist for 30 years and one of my sons-in-law is a career Navy nuclear submariner. Therefore, I know a little about what it means to be a soldier. I also know that the men and women who serve you and me in this way have each answered a "call" to serve, protect, and defend their country. With a lot at stake and with tremendous sacrifices, they have raised a hand, signed on, stepped across a line, all in order to fight for us and for our country.

Well, my dear sister-in-Christ, God is asking you to answer His call and join His army of prayer "warriors." No, He's not asking us to give our physical lives…but He is asking us to give our *spiritual* lives in the service of prayer in order to fight for and serve, protect, and defend our families, friends, churches, nations, and His people on the battle line of prayer. God is asking us to answer His call to pray. He is asking us to make a deep, serious, spiritual commitment to pray, to raise our hand, to sign on, to step across a line, to fight for Him and His causes…through prayer.

God speaks in His Word of your "sacrifice" of "service" (Romans 12:1). And just as a soldier does not allow anything to hinder his or her commitment to serve, neither can you. That means that worldliness, busyness, and foolishness must all be dealt with. These deterrents to prayer must not be allowed to come between you and your "service" of prayer to God and for your loved ones and others.

Prayer is a high calling, for sure. And remember, our greatest service will come with the greatest sacrifice. But oh, what a high calling it is! Now, what will your answer to God's call to prayer be?

Prayer is one way God has provided
for us to commune with Him,
and when we accept His invitation
to commune with Him,
He will transform our hearts
and change our lives.

—ELIZABETH GEORGE

Ten Reasons Women Don't Pray—Part 2

I'm sure you've learned many skills in your lifetime. And I was recently reminded of one of mine while spending a New York Thanksgiving in my daughter Katherine's home. One evening Kath pulled out her newest undertaking—knitting! I was absolutely overjoyed as memories came flooding back to me, delightful memories of the days of learning to knit one, purl one, and to cast off. Because of a desire to learn, a decision to learn, and a determination to learn, in time and through practice—years of practice!—the skill became mine until it was so ingrained that I could knit without even looking at the needles.

Well, my companion-in-prayer, learning to pray is no different than learning to knit...or learning any other skill. You and I must *desire* to pray, *decide* to pursue it, *determine* to keep at it, and, of course, *do* it!

And in the case of prayer, we must also *defend* our desire, our decision, our determination, and our diligence in doing the work of prayer. We must watch out for any hindrances that even *might* keep us from prayer, from answering God's call to us to pray and making prayer a reality in our lives.

We've already noted three possible reasons we sometimes fail to pray—worldliness, busyness, and foolishness. Now let's identify several others.

4. *Distance*—If you know people well, you can usually talk easily with them. But you probably have difficulty talking to a stranger. And the same thing happens in our communication with God. When you and I don't have a close enough relationship with God, we find it hard to "talk" to Him. So the solution is obvious—we must begin "talking" to God through prayer. We must actively seek to close any gaps in distance that may have developed. As a favorite verse instructs, "draw near to God and He will draw near to you" (James 4:8).

What are some of the things that can create distance in our bond with God? Here are a few answers: Neglect. Bitterness. Laziness. Procrastination. Sin. Distractions. Pride. I'm sure you could add to this list. Just think about any friendship...or former friendship...you once enjoyed that isn't as close as it used to be. Then ask, "What happened?"

Well, dear one, the same can prove true in our relationship and intimacy with God if we don't keep making the effort to pray. So, if for *any* reason you've been putting off talking to God through prayer, make a step—*now!*—to reconnect. Do what you must to reopen the lines of communication. It's urgent! So don't put it off. God hasn't changed, disappeared, or withdrawn His care and concern for you or stopped listening to you. No, the fault is always with you and me.

Therefore, close the gap. Draw near to God. Simply take a step in prayer—any step!—that will begin to eliminate any distance that has impaired your rapport with your heavenly Father. He's waiting for you.

5. *Ignorance*—We don't understand or grasp God's goodness or His desire and ability to provide for us "exceedingly abundantly" (Ephesians 3:20) and to "supply all our need" (Philippians 4:19). Therefore, we don't ask or pray.

Yet the truth is that God wants to grant our requests, to give us the desires of our hearts, and to bless us. It is His nature. As Jesus Himself taught,

> What man is there among you who, if his son asks for bread, will give him a stone? Or if he asks for a fish, will he give him a serpent? If you then, being evil, know how to give good gifts to your children, *how much more* will your Father who is in heaven give good things to those who ask Him! (Matthew 7:9-11).

God is good. And God is a giving God. But God also wants us to ask Him. In the words of Charles Spurgeon, famed preacher-of-old, "Whether we like it or not, asking is the rule of the Kingdom."

- "Call to Me, and I will answer you, and show you great and mighty things, which you do not know" (Jeremiah 33:3).

- "You ask and do not receive because you ask amiss" (James 4:3).

❧   "Ask, and it will be given to you...for everyone who asks receives" (Matthew 7:7-8).

Dear one, answer God's call to pray and start asking. Ask boldly and fervently for the salvation of your loved ones and friends (James 5:16). Ask earnestly for God's will as you make decisions (Acts 9:6). Ask for your daily needs (Matthew 6:11). Cultivate the childlike faith of the little boy who, ready for bed, came in to announce to his family in the living room, "I'm going to say my prayers now. Anybody want anything?"

6. *Sinfulness*—We don't pray because we know we have sinned against our holy God. Adam and Eve, who enjoyed a relationship with God no human has known since—a perfect relationship!—hid themselves from God after they sinned (Genesis 3:8). And King David, after his adulterous affair with Bathsheba and after arranging for the murder of her husband, ceased praying and "kept silent" (Psalm 32:3).

So what is the solution to our sinfulness? David instructs us to acknowledge it. "I will confess my transgressions to the Lord" (verse 5). James says, "Confess your trespasses" (James 5:16). John echoes James and exhorts us to "confess our sins" (1 John 1:9). And Jesus instructed us to pray to God, asking Him to *forgive us our debts*, our trespasses and offenses, the wrong we have done (Matthew 6:12).

And then what happens? The floodgates of communion with God are opened once again. As David expressed it, he was once again "clean,...whiter than snow." He also heard anew the sounds of joy and gladness. He experienced afresh the joy of his salvation (see Psalm 51:7-12).

So, as women who are called to righteousness, godliness, faith, love...and prayer, we must not deny our sin, nor blame others for it, nor hide it, nor rationalize it. It was David himself who declared to God in his brokenness, "Against You, You only, have I sinned, and done this evil in Your sight" (Psalm 51:4).

Oh, dear friend, we simply cannot forfeit our ability and our opportunity to pray for ourselves, our family and friends, and those in need because we are too proud or stubborn to deal with sin. Too much is at stake—and at risk—to hold on to secret or favorite sins. Keep short accounts with God when it comes to sin. And what is the best way to treat sin? I've often been advised to deal with any sin as it comes up— on the spot! At the exact minute that I slip up and fail!

Remember, the Bible teaches us that it is the "effective, fervent prayer of a *righteous* man [or woman that] avails much" (James 5:16). In other words, the prayer of an upright, godly man or woman—the one who seeks to walk in obedience, who confesses and forsakes sin (Proverbs 28:13)— brings powerful results.

Checklist for Prayer

✓ *Examine your relationship with God*—Harder than the practical exercises we've encountered regarding worldliness, busyness, and foolishness is the spiritual exercise of examining your relationship with your heavenly Father. So first of all, ask yourself, "Am I praying regularly?" If your answer is *yes,* praise God…and continue on in your faithfulness. However, if your answer is *no,* ask "Why? What happened?" Then run through the list of reasons below and circle the culprit that is robbing you of tending to your relationship and friendship with God. Identify the

Number One excuse you are allowing to keep you from prayer.

neglect	bitterness
laziness	procrastination
sin	distractions
pride	other reasons

I'm sure you know the next step: Stop right now, bow your head and your heart in humility before God, acknowledge your wrongful failure to pray to Him...and then pray! (Now, where did you put that kitchen timer?) Remember, He's waiting for you!

✓ *Write out verses to memorize*—Begin with Jeremiah 33:3, James 4:3, and Matthew 7:7-8. Have you failed in your previous efforts to memorize Scripture? Let me share these surefire aids with you:

Write the verses on cards,
Write them out ten times, and
Write them on the tablet of your heart.

By having your verses on cards, you are *seeing* them. By writing them out ten times with pen and paper, you are *touching* them. And by writing them "on the tablet of your heart" (Proverbs 3:3)—by saying them over and over, you are *internalizing* them until they become yours.

As you follow these three "write" ways to memorize the three verses about God's desire and ability to answer your prayers, you'll surely overcome your hesitance to just ask!

✓   *Search your heart for sin*—Look for past or present sin
     that needs to be acknowledged and taken care of.
     David, who was ravaged by the consequences of his
     personal sin, instructs us here. He prayed, "Examine
     me, O LORD, and prove me; try my mind and my
     heart....Search me, O God, and know my heart...and
     see if there is any wicked way in me" (Psalm 26:2 and
     139:23-24). David, who had been burned by his own
     unconfessed sin, invited God's scrutiny of every corner
     of his life.

Answering God's Call to You

These three hindrances to prayer—distance,
ignorance, and sinfulness—have taken us much
deeper into ourselves, haven't they? In them we've
been forced to face our sinful hearts.

Think about it. Worldliness, busyness, and foolishness are really very minor distractions in our
quest to be women of prayer...when laid beside
these three new deterrents, aren't they? The first
assortment of reasons for failing to pray have to do
with carelessness and oversight. We live in the
world, we have work to do, and none of us will-
fully decides to be a fool or to act foolishly. We just
neglect to give attention to these prayer robbers.

But in distance, ignorance, and sinfulness...well,
we have suddenly stepped into a more serious and
dangerous realm of hindrances. You see, these hindrances are more willful. In them we are actually

choosing to keep God at arm's length. We are choosing to "pass" on attempting to understand the magnitude of *God's desire to hear* our prayers and *God's ability to answer* our prayers. And sadly, we are selfishly choosing to sin and forfeit an open channel for interceding for others, not to mention personally enjoying God's rich blessings.

So dear one, do you truly want to answer God's call to prayer? Do you really want to make your desire to pray a reality in your life? Then, precious sister...

> ...to guard against distance, stay close to God,

> ...to guard against ignorance, stay close to God's Word so you have a better understanding of how you should be praying, and

> ...to guard against sinfulness, stay close to God by pursuing a godly life.

Please, don't allow any cooling off toward your Savior to occur in your heart. The apostle John couldn't get close enough to His beloved Savior and Friend, to God. So he got as close as he could—he leaned on Jesus' breast! Follow in John's steps and stay close to God. Get as close as you can!

God is calling you to a life of prayer. Do answer the call! A more meaningful prayer-life awaits you.

If you want a life of prayer,
the way to get it is
by praying.

—THOMAS MERTON

Ten Reasons Women Don't Pray–Part 3

*H*ow are you doing on making your desire to pray a reality? Have you found any of your pet excuses for not praying in our inventory of reasons? I know all of these barriers to prayer have been problems for me. I can personally claim every one of them because, as I said before, I am the author of this awful list! So you know that I can definitely relate to you and your struggles. In fact, all Christians can identify with you because "no temptation has overtaken you except such as is *common* to man" (1 Corinthians 10:13).

Oh, how I hope and pray you are being honest. For to heed God's call to prayer requires that we check our progress and identify any problems. I also hope and pray you are following through on the steps at the end of each chapter to turn any faults and failures around.

And now, let's complete the list. We're almost at the finish line! There are a few more reasons that keep God's people from fulfilling their desire to answer His call to prayer.

7. *Faithlessness*—We don't really believe in the power of prayer. We don't think that prayer makes any difference. We don't believe that things might have different outcomes due to faithful and earnest prayer...therefore we don't pray.

And yet our Lord taught that when you and I ask according to His will, "whatever things you ask in prayer, *believing*, you will receive" (Matthew 21:22). Enjoy the devotional thought that follows regarding this wonderful promise from Jesus...and then, in faith and by faith, draw the bow, shoot the arrow, and in prayer send your heart's message upward to heaven!

> Prayer is the bow,
>> the promise is the arrow:
>>> faith is the hand which draws the bow, and sends the arrow with the heart's message to heaven.
> The bow without the arrow is of no use; and
>> the arrow without the bow is of little worth; and
>>> both, without the strength of the hand, to no purpose.
> Neither the promise without prayer,
>> nor prayer without the promise,
>>> nor both without faith,
>>>> avail the Christian anything.
> What was said of the Israelites, "They could not enter in, because of unbelief,"
>> the same may be said of many of our prayers: they cannot enter heaven, because they are not put up in faith.[1]

8. *Pridefulness*—Prayer reflects our dependence on God. When we fail to pray, we are saying that we don't have any

needs...or worse, that we are choosing not to ask the one Person who can help us. Our prayerlessness defiantly declares, "I'll take care of it myself, thank You!" However, God calls out, "If My people who are called by My name will humble themselves, and pray and seek My face, and turn from their wicked ways, then I will hear from heaven" (2 Chronicles 7:14).

So let's be quick to humble ourselves and pray and seek God's glorious face. Let's turn fully away from our "wicked ways" and enjoy the sunshine of His grace. Let's again take a page out of David's prayer book and pray, "Search me, O God...and see if there is any wicked way in me" (Psalm 139:23-24).

It's a fact—true, earnest prayer and pride cannot exist in the same place at the same time. Therefore, "the self-sufficient do not pray, the self-satisfied will not pray, the self-righteous cannot pray."[2] May you and I, as women of God, fail to qualify in any of these three prideful categories! May we instead enjoy the blessings that come from cultivating a humble heart: "The LORD is near to those who have a broken heart, and saves such as have a contrite spirit" (Psalm 34:18).

9. *Inexperience*—We don't pray because we don't pray! And because we don't pray, we don't know how to pray...so we don't pray. It's a vicious cycle. Yet prayer, like any skill, becomes easier with repetition. The more we pray, the more we know how to pray. And the more we know how to pray, the more we pray. It's as simple as that.

And in case you are feeling like you are the only person who ever lived who's had difficulty praying, I want to quickly remind you that even those closest to Jesus—His disciples—had the same problem. They watched Jesus pray.

They heard Jesus pray. They even heard Jesus pray for them! Finally they went to the Master Pray-er Himself and asked, "Lord, teach us to pray" (Luke 11:1).

Pray this same prayer for yourself, dear one. Pray, "Lord, teach *me* to pray!" But also take the first (or rusty, as the case may be!) step and start praying...and keep praying. Break the cycle! Even if you don't know what you are doing or fear you are doing it badly, pray anyway. As one person wisely observed,

> If we are willing to take hours on end to learn to play the piano, or operate a computer, or fly an airplane, it is sheer nonsense for us to imagine that we can learn the high art of getting guidance through communion with the Lord without being willing to set aside time for it. It is no accident that the Bible speaks of prayer as a form of waiting on God.[3]

So pray! Pray purposefully, regularly, diligently, and faithfully. In time...and through persistence...you will begin to feel more comfortable and familiar with the spiritual endeavor of prayer. You will begin to experience and enjoy your priceless privilege of communicating with the God of the universe!

10. *Laziness*—You and I can fully grasp and admit that the nine obstacles to a powerful prayer life that we've addressed to this point are prayer killers. We can agree that worldliness, busyness, foolishness, distance, and ignorance will definitely thwart our prayer efforts. And we can heartily concur that sinfulness, faithlessness, pridefulness, and inexperience will impede our progress in personally answering

God's call to prayer. But even if we overcome these nine reasons for not praying, this tenth one—laziness—will make us or break us in the Prayer Department!

I'm sure I don't have to paint a picture for you of the lifestyle of laziness. (We've both been there and done that, right?) But one example is the woman who can't get to bed at night because of snacking on junk food…or junk TV…or the junk offered on the internet (or all of the above). Then guess what? She can't get up in the morning to meet with the Lord and pray about her life, her purpose, her goals, her character, her precious family members! And all day long she can't get going, runs behind, or worse, gives up and gives in again to both physical and spiritual laziness.

As I said, I've been there and done that! And it took the faithful mentoring of a godly woman and tremendous effort on my part—and God's amazing grace!—to break some life-long habits that were thwarting my desire to be a woman of prayer and robbing me of the time I needed to become such a woman. Two things, two *simple* acts, helped me move forward in conquering laziness.

First, I put my personal principle of "head for bed" into action as soon as the evening meal was done and the kitchen cleaned up. No, that doesn't mean that I went to bed at six o'clock. But it does mean that at six o'clock I began to get my daughters bathed and into their pajamas. I would also shut down the house, wash my face and brush my teeth, check the schedule for the next day and begin a to-do list, and get into my own pj's. Then I set out my prayer notebook and Bible in the place where I would (Lord willing!) have my devotions the next morning. In other words, I was on a mission—to get to bed as soon as I could, as early as possible. I still to this day practice this "head for bed" principle every evening.

Second, I put my prayer principle of "something is better than nothing" to work for me when it was actually time to pray. I had to dispel the myth of the desired and hoped for "sweet hour of prayer" and try for something more manageable and realistic for successfully getting the discipline of daily prayer into place. Then, in time, as I began to taste the sweet fruits of time spent in prayer with my heavenly Father, I graduated little by little to greater lengths of time spent on bended knee.

Checklist for Prayer

✓ *Access your faith-quotient*—Do you believe God answers prayer? Or do you fall into the category of those Jesus addressed as "O you of little faith"? Every Christian's faith can stand to grow even stronger, so determine to pray *no matter what*. And keep records. Many people keep meticulous financial records. They carefully and faithfully watch over their money and their investments, watching and waiting for pay-offs and dividends. Well, I want you to do the same with your "prayer investment." Do as David, a great pray-er and man of faith, did: Pray. Then watch and see what God will do. David prayed and then announced, "I will look up" (Psalm 5:3). In other words, he expected God to act and to answer, so he was going to be on the lookout.

Are you praying for someone? Call the person and get a report. Ask, "What happened?" Then write it down. Keep faithful records of God's faithfulness. Then watch your faith in His faithfulness soar!

And if all else fails, pray, "Lord…help my unbelief" (Mark 9:24)!

✓ *Take time to think*—Really think about what keeps you from praying. Hold each of these ten reasons for failing to pray up to God in prayer. Lay your soul before God, and submit your heart to Him for scrutiny.

For instance, ask in prayer, "God, is there too much of the world in my life and not enough of You? Am I like Martha, too focused on the busy details of daily life and failing to see the big picture, the necessity of prayer? Am I living out the definition of a fool by allowing what is insignificant to rob me of *the* most significant use of my time—time spent praying about my life? Have I allowed anything to create a distance between us, Lord?"

Keep on looking…and keep on praying! "Father, am I neglecting to ask of You in prayer because of a failure to understand Your magnanimous nature? Or is it due to some area of sin in my life that I'm refusing to deal with? Or is my failure to pray a faith issue, a lack of trust? Or pride? Or do I just plain ole don't know how…or am I just plain ole lazy?"

Go ahead and make your way through the ten reasons we've addressed. Perhaps you'll discover other excuses for just plain ole not praying. I'm a firm believer in the expression, "A problem defined is a problem half solved." So it's a good thing to put your finger on the problem so you and the Lord can begin working on a solution!

✓   *Desire to answer God's call*—In almost every interview I participate in on radio or television, I'm usually asked, "Elizabeth, what is one step a woman can take today to begin making this [whatever the subject is] a reality in her life?" And my answer is always the same, no matter what the subject, topic, or discipline—"She must desire it!" (whatever *it* is, which in the case of this book, is to *pray*, to be a woman of prayer, to answer God's call to pray).

You see, you and I can know we need to pray, and we can learn the skills involved in praying. Yet, if we never *desire* to pray, our knowledge and skills mean nothing. Praying will never become a habit or a discipline because the one main ingredient is missing. My friend, it's imperative that we *desire* to pray!

Answering God's Call to You

We've spent a great deal of time, space, and effort looking at the reasons you and I don't pray. So now we wonder, How does a woman after God's own heart—you!—answer God's high calling to pray? Believe it or not, it's not as difficult as you think. Once you begin to eliminate and tend to the issues that keep you from praying...

> Prayer is so simple;
> It is like quietly opening a door
> And slipping into the very
>   presence of God,
> There is the stillness
> To listen to His voice;
> Perhaps to petition,
> Or only to listen:
> It matters not.
> Just to be there
> In His presence
> Is prayer.[4]

Now, won't you slip into the very presence of God? He's waiting for you!

Praying from the Heart

*Lingering in God's presence will
increase our faith,
provide a place for us to unload our burdens,
remind us that God is always near, and
help us not to panic.*

—ELIZABETH GEORGE

5

When You Are in Trouble...Pray!

What is prayer? While researching this far-reaching question, I found these insightful words that begin to give us an answer. Referring to prayer as the pathway to the heart of God, author Terry Glaspey writes,

> To ask the question, "What is prayer?" is to ask a question of such depth that it is beyond our limited human understanding to ever fully answer. The question probes not only the mysteries of what it means to be a human being, but even inquires into the mystery of God Himself.... Because it is a topic too deep for the human intellect, it requires that we look to God as our teacher.[1]

This is exactly what you and I must do right now. We must look to God's Word—the Bible—for *His* definition of prayer, while at the same time acknowledging that prayer lies in the depths of "the mystery of God Himself." As the great apostle and pray-er Paul hopelessly—and worshipfully—exulted when he gave up trying to understand God's actions, "Oh, the depth of the riches both of the wisdom and knowledge of God! How unsearchable are His judgments and His ways past finding out!" (Romans 11:33).

As we look now at prayer as explained by God through the language in the Bible, keep in mind that prayer has, from the very first of time, been the principle means by which man, created in God's image, has evidenced sentiment toward Him. From the earliest times, prayer has been an integral part of the worship of God. Believers of all ages have expressed the feelings and dispositions of their hearts in praise, thanksgiving, prayer, and intercession to and before God. That's why it is so important for God's people to learn to pray. We need to grasp God's instructions for prayer. And we must seek with all our heart, soul, strength, and mind to answer His call to pray.

As we consider prayer's many avenues and concerns, we realize that prayer is like a gem with many facets, each one being admirable, brilliant, skillfully crafted, and contributing to the grandeur of the whole.

In Times of Trouble...Pray!

Here's a word for prayer you're probably familiar with—*supplication*. As one well-loved verse instructs, "Be anxious for nothing, but in everything by prayer and *supplication*, with thanksgiving, let your requests be made known to God" (Philippians 4:6). Clearly we are to ask God in supplication. This term for prayer stems from a Hebrew word that is connected with judges and judging. It means to invoke God as a judge. And to do so means that we must come to Him, *the* Judge! We are to implore *Him* for our needs. And we are to do so earnestly and humbly.

Queen Esther faced trouble. Are you acquainted with the story of Queen Esther? If so, then you know that she practiced *supplication*. And her brave act teaches us something about supplication in prayer. Here's what happened...

In order to save the lives of God's people, Esther had to risk her life by approaching her husband, the king. However, coming uninvited into the presence of the king was punishable by death...and Esther hadn't been summoned. Therefore, Esther fasted for three days and nights before she acted. Then, and only then, did God's courageous heroine humbly draw near to the only person who could possibly intervene and judge on behalf of her and her people, the Jews, and rescue and save their lives. The Scriptures report that Esther went "in to the king to make *supplication* to him and plead before him for her people" (Esther 4:8).

And the end of the story? God went to work in the shadows of the night and set in motion a series of events that led to the salvation of His people!

King Hezekiah faced trouble. Hezekiah, king of Judah, gives us an example of someone humbly beseeching God in supplication. Sennacherib, ruler of Assyria, sent a letter to King Hezekiah threatening him and reproaching "the living God," whom Hezekiah served. What did the king do? Answer: Hezekiah "spread it before the LORD" and asked in supplication for God's intervention. He pleaded, "O LORD, our God, I pray, save us from his hand" (2 Kings 19:19).

And the end of the story? The answer to Hezekiah's prayers of supplication? God Himself said, "*I* will defend this city, to save it for *My* own sake and for *My* servant David's sake" (verse 34).

And we can't stop there! The next verse reports, "And it came to pass on a certain night that the angel of the LORD went out, and killed in the camp of the Assyrians one hundred and eighty-five thousand; and when people arose early in the morning, there were the corpses—all dead" (verse 35).

Now, *that's* an answer to prayer!

Jesus spoke of trouble. Jesus also points us to prayer in times of trouble. He "spoke a parable...that men always ought to pray and not lose heart" (Luke 18:1) or "faint" (KJV). Praying instead of fainting refers to the words, attitude, and devotion of supplication that looks expectantly to God in times of trouble. Such prayer keeps us from *caving in.* And what causes a cave-in? Answer: Weakness on one hand and pressure on another. When the going gets rough, we're not to faint, lose heart, give in, give up, and cave in. Instead we are to pray, to ask God in supplication, to trust Him and move forward. It's true that "he stands best who kneels most." And, dear heart, we can always pray in helplessness when we can't do anything else! That's what supplication is. So put this prayer-weapon to good use in your times of trouble.

I once heard a story about a young boy who was saved from drowning by his brother and carried home unconscious by his group of friends. The grateful father wanted to know exactly who had done what so that he could properly thank each child. So he said to John...

"Well, John, what did you do?"

He replied, "Oh, I jumped into the water and pulled him out!"

"And James and Thomas, what did you do?" questioned the dad.

"Oh, we carried Danny home!"

"And Mary, what did you do?" came the next inquiry.

And poor little Mary, who was only three years old, burst into tears and said, "Daddy, I couldn't do anything at all, so I just prayed and prayed!"

Then her father gently said, "Mary, you deserve the most praise of all, for you did all you could, and God answered your prayers through John and James and Thomas."

My friend, in times of trouble...when you can't do anything at all...just pray and pray! That's supplication—turning to God in prayer in the tough times, when you don't know where else to go or what else to do.

I have faced trouble. For the past five years I've been working on a new-to-me spiritual discipline—that of keeping a journal. My efforts at journaling are not a tell-all, spill-all kind of recording, but it is a highlight-all account. By that I mean I log dates, events, happenings, and adventures. I can then look back periodically and see the path my life has been on and is taking. All of the highlights are there—the celebration of each personal and family anniversary, the arrival of each new grandbaby, the completion of each new book (whether Jim's or mine), family times together, blessings, accomplishments....Well, you know the list!

But the "low-lights," as well, are entered there in my little leather-bound journal—the lingering afflictions and deaths of both of my sweet parents, the loss of a husband/wife set of best friends within seven weeks of each other, my failures, the hard times of injury, misunderstanding, confusion, disappointment....Well, again you know the list!

And, my dear friend, I've had to learn that just as I praise God profusely for the highlights, I pray to Him profusely, in supplication, concerning the low-lights—the trials, tribulations, and troubles! You see, *He* must fight my battles (Psalm 60:12). *He* must judge and make things right (Psalm 37:6). *He* must act on my behalf (1 Peter 5:6). *He* must deliver me (Psalm 143:9) and help me to go on in the presence of my enemies (Psalm 23:5). And prayer is my way of handling the trouble I cannot handle.

You will face trouble. Trouble is a fact of life. Another truth Jesus spoke informs us that "in the world you *will* have tribulation" (John 16:33). Paul, the great sufferer for Christ, reiterated this reality when he declared that "all who desire to live godly in Christ Jesus *will* suffer persecution" (2 Timothy 3:12).

So...are you still wondering, Why pray? Here's some help with your answer. You are to pray because prayer releases the energy of God, the Judge. And are you wondering, When should I pray? You should pray in times of trouble. And what is prayer? Here's one answer: Prayer is a means of asking God to do what we cannot do. Prayer moves the hand that moves the universe, so you are to pray, to ask God in supplication.

Now, what is troubling you, my precious reading friend? I'm praying for you here in my office as you face your challenges. I'm praying that in your times of trouble you never forget to pray in supplication to your almighty, all-powerful, miracle-working, impossible-mountain-moving God! Don't just stand there! Don't cave in! Don't worry! And don't suffer! "Is anyone among you suffering? Let him *pray*" (James 5:13)!

Checklist for Prayer

✓ *Look at your "Prayer Calendar"*—Remember, one picture is worth a thousand words! Hopefully progress has been made since you began on your fresh commitment to be more faithful in answering God's call to be a woman who makes her desire to pray a reality. (Have you been using your Prayer Calendar? It's not too late to start! Just shade in the dates that you do pray and leave the days blank when you haven't prayed. This will help you track your progress in the discipline of prayer and encourage you to pray more often!)

I hope and pray you are beginning to grasp the importance of a well-ingrained prayer-life. When you are in the habit of praying, you are definitely more likely to pray when trouble arises. And when you are in the habit of praying, you are definitely more likely to think of asking for God's help first instead of later...or last, when all else fails.

If you had to pray about one way to be even more consistent at regular prayer, what change would you make? What could you do that would make all the difference in the world in your prayer-life? Think of that one thing, put it on your personal prayer list, enlist the aid of another person to help you with accountability...and then get to work on kicking your efforts at prayer up a notch!

✓ *Look for trouble*—Remember that trouble is part of the Christian life. A giant growth-step in faith and maturity is to acknowledge, accept, and learn this fact of life. As my Jim always says, "Being a Christian is not a bed of roses!" I know it helped me tremendously to underline in my Bible the little word "when" in James 1:2: "My brethren, count it all joy *when* you fall into various trials." It's quite sobering—and instructive—to realize that James did not say *if*...but he said *when* as he wrote of trials in life.

The apostle Peter, too, wrote of the facts of trials and troubles, exhorting us with these words: "Beloved, do not think it strange concerning the fiery trial which is to try you, as though some strange thing happened to you" (1 Peter 4:12).

You and I, dear one, must face life with our eyes wide open. We must accept the fact of trouble. Then we must devise a plan for handling trouble and for dealing with it—God's way. For instance, what will you think when trouble arrives? What scriptures will you use to stay strong in the Lord as you walk through your own fiery trials? And what, when, and how will you pray about the troubles of life—past, present, and future? Wisdom always has a plan (Proverbs 21:5), so create your plan of action for facing trouble. Be prepared for trouble.

✓   *Look for highlights*—Remember to thank God for His blessings. However, are you presently living in a low-light? Then identify it, touch it, label it, and own it. Determine (with God's help!) that there will be no more denying it or wishing it away. No longer be shocked that it happens. Once again, a problem defined is a problem half solved. So acknowledge your problem because once you have, you can then pray concerning it. And then stand back and wait to behold the goodness of the Lord and see how He chooses to answer your prayers and work on your behalf.

Answering God's Call to You

Now...what should you do when you face trouble?

I hope you noticed the common denominator in the accounts of both Queen Esther's and King Hezekiah's supplications. It was *trouble!* The context of the use of the word "supplication" for prayer is in times of trouble and helplessness.

So I pray God's message to your heart is crystal clear. When you're in trouble...pray! When you're helpless...pray! When you've done all you can do but you're still in need of help...once again, pray! You are to ask God in supplication, dear child of God. God's call and instruction to your heart is to remember to pray in times of trouble. Don't *lose* heart! *Pray* from the heart!

LORD, *make me a channel of Thy peace*
That where there is hatred, I may bring love,
That where there is wrong, I may bring the
   spirit of forgiveness.
That where there is discord, I may bring
   harmony,
That where there is error, I may bring truth,
That where there is doubt, I may bring faith,
That where there is despair, I may bring hope,
That where there are shadows, I may bring
   light,
That where there is sadness, I may bring joy.

—ST. FRANCIS OF ASSISI

6

When You Are Disappointed by Others...Pray!

nce upon a time there was a leader who spent his life teaching God's law and standards to His people. But, sadly, the day came when God assigned this man to speak to the people about their sin. When he confronted the masses with their sinful failure, they were utterly convicted of their wrongdoing and begged the man of God to pray for them.

That man of God was God's prophet Samuel.

The people were God's people, Israel.

The sin they had committed was choosing to have a king to lead them rather than trusting God's direct guidance of them through His prophets (like Samuel!).

And what was Samuel's response to the sinning people's request that he pray for them, the very people who had disappointed not only God, but him, too? Samuel said, "Far be it from me that I should sin against the LORD in ceasing to pray for you" (1 Samuel 12:23).

Pray for Others

This story about Samuel from the pages of Scripture brings us on our journey into prayer to yet another facet in the prized jewel of prayer—that of praying for those who disappoint us in some way. As Christians, we are called to pray for others, including those who have failed us or harmed us.

For instance...

Moses prayed for his brother Aaron...after Aaron disappointed both Moses and God by wrongfully making a golden calf for God's people to worship (Deuteronomy 9:12-20). While Moses was away, Aaron, the high priest of God and Moses' co-leader, had clearly disobeyed the commands of God (Exodus 32:8), and God was on the warpath!

And exactly how mad was God at Aaron? The Bible reports that the Lord was very angry with Aaron and would have destroyed him (verse 19). In other words, Aaron had had it. He was done. There seemed to be no hope for his life. Yet Moses prayed and beseeched God on behalf of his sinning brother.

Moses prayed for God's people...when God turned His holy wrath upon them due to their desire to honor a golden calf instead of worship Him. Moses had faithfully taught the Israelites and led them and prayed for them. And yet they disappointed Moses *and* God!

And exactly how mad was God at His people? God said to Moses, "Let Me alone, that I may destroy them and blot out their name from under heaven" (verse 14). When Moses spoke to the people, he said, "I was afraid of the anger and hot displeasure with which the LORD was angry with you, to destroy you" (verse 19). And Moses went to prayer on their behalf.

Job prayed for his friends... after God turned His judgment upon Job's peers when His wrath was kindled against them for wrongfully charging His servant Job with sin. Yet Job, after receiving much criticism from these same close companions, was able to pray for them (Job 42:8). In fact, God sent the sinning trio of friends *to* Job, saying, "Go to My servant Job...and My servant Job shall pray for you...lest I deal with you according to your folly" (verse 8). And Job prayed for them.

A question or two for you—Could...and would...you have done what Moses did for his brother Aaron, who knew better than to sin in the way that he did? And would you have been able to do for "friends" what Job did for his, to pray for them...after they had disappointed you, turned on you, let you down, and raked you over the coals in wrongful judgment?

I'm sure you can already discern that to pray for those who fail to obey God *and* disappoint and harm you takes a special kind of person...with a special heart. We'll look at the elements of soul that make us the kind of people who can continue to pray for those who disappoint us and others in a little bit. But what is important right now is grasping the meaning, the honor, the privilege, the seriousness, the duty—and the difficulty!—of this marvelous call to pray for others when they fail.

When You Are Disappointed by Others...
Forgive One Another!

You probably agree—and know from firsthand experience—that it's extremely difficult to forgive people who have failed you as a friend or who have inaccurately accused you of wrongdoing. But surely Samuel *forgave* God's people ...and prayed for them. Surely Moses *forgave* his brother and God's people...and prayed for them. And surely Job *forgave* his critical friends...and prayed for them. How else could these men have earnestly and wholeheartedly prayed for others if they had not first forgiven them? As Psalm 66:18 explains regarding prayer, "If I regard iniquity in my heart, the Lord will not hear."

And the same is true for you and me. If we fail to forgive, we become unable to pray due to the sin of failing to forgive. We can carry a grudge toward a person, allowing bitterness or resentment to take root in our hearts (Hebrews 12:15). And once such sins become a part of our life, we forfeit the opportunity to minister to that person through prayer. As Proverbs 28:9 states, "One who turns away his ear from hearing the law, even his prayer is an abomination." Therefore our hearts must be right before God in order to forgive and pray for those who sin, who fail, and who disappoint us (James 5:16).

Our natural tendency is to write off those we are disenchanted with—to no longer have anything to do with them, to distance ourselves from them. But God's Word has a word for us here. We are to be "forgiving one another, even as God in Christ forgave [us]" (Ephesians 4:32; Colossians 3:13). So we forgive...and we pray. Jesus shows us the better way, the right way, *His* way, of dealing with those who disappoint us. He says we are to *pray* for them (Luke 6:28).

So be careful, dear heart! When it comes to praying for others, there cannot be a personal agenda. And there can be no personal accounting system of wrongs (1 Corinthians 13:5). We are simply to forgive and to pray to God on their behalf. This takes a great deal of maturity. But a clean heart toward God (Psalm 51:7 and 10) and toward the offender prepares the way for praying from the heart in a hurtful situation.

When You Are Disappointed by Others... Watch Your Heart!

I hope you are wondering, What kind of heart did each of these three powerful pray-ers—Samuel, Moses, and Job—possess? How can I follow their godly example? And what kind of person must I seek to become in order to pray for those who have failed and/or hurt or disappointed me? Well, let's see.

Samuel, the prophet, priest, and judge whom God had designated and established to lead His people (1 Samuel 3:20), had been soundly rejected by the people of Israel. They had virtually ejected Samuel from his God-ordained office of leadership. Yet in spite of their many unkindnesses and their ingratitude, Samuel could still pray for them because of his selflessness and his forgiving spirit. His heart was pure and right before God...and toward the people. Therefore he could pray to God for them from his heart. His attitude was one of, "Pray for you? Yes, to my latest breath! God forbid that I should sin against the Lord in ceasing to pray for you."[1]

Moses, the leader of God's people, was away when they sinned against God and "cast a stain upon the divine glory by the molten calf" they desired to worship.[2] And where was Moses? He was fasting forty days and nights on Mount Sinai.

When Moses returned from the mount, he saw the people's sin. And what was his response? He "fell down before the LORD," explaining "for I was afraid...so I prayed" (Deuteronomy 9:18-20). (And just a note—Moses "fell down before the LORD" and prayed and fasted before God on behalf of the sinful people for 40 *more* days and nights!)

And what did Moses pray? "Oh, these people have committed a great sin...yet now, if You will forgive their sin—but if not, I pray, blot *me* out of Your book which You have written" (Exodus 32:31-32). In other words, Moses was willing to offer up not only fasting and prayers on behalf of the people, but also his life rather than see them rejected, disowned, and destroyed.

Job, the "blameless and upright" Job who "feared God and shunned evil" (Job 1:1), was attacked by his "friends" at the same time he was enduring the loss of basically all that he had—family, health, and wealth. Yet Job was patient. And Job was humble. And finally it was God Himself who intervened and put an end to Job's friends' inaccurate accusations and speculations as to why Job was suffering. And then the righteous—and honorable!—Job prayed for his friends.

Oh, how I pray that you and I, as women who are called to pray, will follow in the honorable, righteous, forgiving footsteps of these three who belonged to God's noble army of intercessors and pray-ers! Because their hearts were clean, guileless, right, praying, and forgiving, they could pray for others...even those who had disappointed or personally harmed them.

When You Are Disappointed by Others...
Offer a Helping Hand!

As a young child, I remember my mother reading a particular fable to me. While she read, I studied the painting in our storybook that illustrated the fable. It pictured a man who was frantically calling out for help while he was drowning in a river. On the footbridge that spanned the water, another man was casually leaning over the rail looking at the struggling man.

According to the story, the observer was lecturing the man who was drowning beneath him, telling him what he *ought* to have done and letting him know what he *should* do if he ever got into that situation again. Instead of reaching in with a helping hand and saving the dying man's life, he talked on and on about what the man who had fallen into the water had done wrong and how he could avoid the same mistake in the future. Clearly the perishing man didn't need a lecture! He needed help! He needed someone to save his life!

And that, dear reader and helper-of-others, is what you and I have to do when it comes to praying for those who have fallen and failed. We must help them! We must set aside our disappointment, forsake the lectures, forsake the judgment, forsake the shock, and go to work helping and praying for others, taking heed *lest we fall* (1 Corinthians 10:12). Sure, correction, instruction, restoration, and rebuilding may come later. But when a person has failed and is in trouble, we are to pray and offer a helping hand.

And here's another tip for dealing with those who have fallen: "If a man is overtaken in any trespass, you who are spiritual restore such a one in a spirit of gentleness, considering yourself *lest you also be tempted*" (Galatians 6:1).

Checklist for Prayer

✓ *Check your prayer-life*—Are you praying regularly? Daily? The person who prays faithfully is more likely to pray for others. Prayer is the sacred act that helps keep your heart pure and right, guileless and humble, no matter what a person has done to harm or disappoint you. Don't find yourself disqualified and unable to pray for others when there is a critical need because you haven't been nursing your prayer-life…and your heart.

✓ *Check your heart*—Is there anyone you are failing to forgive? A forgiving heart is a heart that can pray for others. And if you think you can't forgive someone, consider the sobering messages of these truths to your heart: "For all have sinned and fall short of the glory of God….Let him who thinks he stands take heed lest he fall….If we say that we have no sin, we deceive ourselves, and the truth is not in us."[3]

Rm 3:23   I co 10:12   I Joh 1:8

✓ *Check your relationships*—Again, Christ calls you to love others—even your enemies! His instructions concerning those who have wronged you come from Luke 6:27-28:

> *Love* your enemies,
> *do good* to those who hate you,
> *bless* those who curse you, and
> *pray for* those who spitefully use you.

Are you doing kind deeds for those who have harmed you or let you down? Are you speaking kind words to and about those who have slandered or verbally attacked you? And are you praying for those who have hurt or disappointed you? Look to God for His most able and gracious help, and then do what He says you must do to love your enemies.

Answering God's Call to You

Samuel, Moses, Job—and you, dear one? Could your name be added to such a list of pray-ers? Of forgivers? Of pure-hearted intercessors? Of helpers?

Beloved, that's God's call to you. You are to pray for others...period. You are to pray for those you love...and for those who don't love you. You are to pray for those you appreciate...and for those who have disappointed you and failed in their love. You are to pray for those who faithfully serve God...and for those who have stumbled in their walk with Him. You are to "bear one another's burdens, and so fulfill the law of Christ" (Galatians 6:2). What a high calling!

The secret prayer chamber is a
bloody battleground.
Here violent and decisive battles are fought out.
Here the fate of souls
for time and eternity is determined,
in quietude and solitude.[1]

—O. HALLESBY

When You Are Hurting...Pray!

ne of my favorite words in the English language is "bittersweet." Its use never fails to make me think of the well-known announcement, "I've got good news and bad news. Which do you want first?" This picturesque term also reminds me that many occurrences in life fall simultaneously into the glad–sad category, bringing forth both emotions at once.

We wonder, How can something be both bitter and sweet at once? It can only be so because of God's great power and grace! As you have probably already experienced, it is God and God alone who is able to sweeten what is bitter (Exodus 15:23-25), to make the one who is sad become glad (Psalm 30:11), and to turn something bad into something good (Romans 8:28).

Now, the next question is, How can God do this for you and me? How can we have our personal sorrows and injuries, our emotional hurts and pains, transformed from something bitter into something at least bittersweet?

And the answer, precious sister, is...

When Your Heart Hurts...Pray!

Yet another facet in the treasured gem of prayer that we're admiring in this book is our privilege to *contend* in prayer. When we have been harmed by someone, when our heart hurts because of betrayal or injustice or unrighteousness, we are to *contend* in prayer.

Picture this. "To contend" means to stretch or to strive in opposition against evil and for righteousness. In other words, the one who contends goes to battle, wages war, clashes heads for right versus wrong. Therefore, to contend in prayer means we have to maintain, to assert, to "argue" (as it were) with God against evil and for righteousness. We become the literal, living, praying definition of what it means to be a "prayer-warrior."

Meet someone whose heart was hurt—Meet David, a warrior and a king—*and* a prayer-warrior! In one of his psalms (Psalm 55), David poured out his torn and bleeding heart on paper and cried out to God against his enemies. This psalm is entitled by one noted Bible scholar in a single tell-all word—"Betrayed."[2] In it David prays—*contends*—in complaint against false friends.

The background of this psalm is absolutely heartbreaking. Jerusalem, "the city of David," was rebelliously occupied by Absalom, David's own son. Adding insult to injury, Ahithophel, David's close friend, confidant, and a member of his cabinet, turned his loyalty away from David to follow David's upstart son. On top of such treachery, the people of the city also rebelled against David's leadership and ousted him. In fact, seven terms are used in this psalm to describe the wickedness of the city-gone-mad: violence and strife, iniquity and trouble, destruction, oppression, and deceit.

Are you someone who's been hurt?—As I'm sitting here at my desk reading from a dozen or so textbooks, I am thinking of you, dear heart. I'm wondering, Are you someone who's been hurt? Not one day goes by that I don't receive a letter or an email from a woman like you who has been hurt in untold ways by others. I know firsthand that people hurt people. I also know that God's people hurt God's people. And I'm aware that family members hurt family members...and the list goes on. My heart is crying out with James, "These things ought not to be so" (James 3:10), yet I know full well that these things *are so!*

So what are we, as God's women, to do when our hearts hurt and when we've been hurt by evil, by some wrongdoing, by loved ones, friends, family, by those we revered and respected, by those we trusted?

The answer, of course, is...*pray!* And the disheartened David shows us how.

Lessons on Praying from a Hurting Heart

Dare to step now into the heart-wrenching cries of Psalm 55. It contains oh-so-much instruction for our own hurting, bewildered hearts! Here we learn lessons for living life and about praying from the wounded heart and prayer of David, a prayer-warrior. Evil, unrighteousness, and stinging treachery, along with David's grievous personal agony, caused him to cry out and contend with God:

> Give ear to my prayer, O God, and do not hide
> Yourself from my supplication. Attend to me, and
> hear me; I am restless in my complaint, and moan
> noisily….My heart is severely pained within me,
> and the terrors of death have fallen upon me (see
> verses 1-2,4).

Lesson #1—Cast your burden on the Lord. First note that
David knew *where* to turn and *what* to do. He knew to cast
his burden upon the Lord. And you and I, too, have an
almighty and all-loving Father who offers to help us and sustain us to carry our loads. "He who watched over the infant
deliverer of Israel in his cradle of rushes, who sent His
ravens to feed Elijah by the brookside, who protected Daniel
in the lion's den, and kept Paul calm and cheerful in the
hurricane, is the very One who says to us—roll your anxieties over on Me, for I have you in My heart!"[3]

Lesson #2—Resist the temptation to run away. David's
natural desire was to leave the scene, to flee from the
problem and the pain, to get out of harm's way. (Who
wouldn't have this desire!) Perhaps he thought, "No way am
I going to stand here and take this. I'm out of here! I don't
need this!" So David wished for wings!

> Oh, that I had wings like a dove! I would fly
> away and be at rest. Indeed, I would wander far
> off, and remain in the wilderness….I would
> hasten my escape from the windy storm and tem-
> pest (verses 6-8).

Beloved, when you find yourself surrounded by enemies
or suffering due to the deceit and failure of your friends,

you will most certainly sigh for the wings of a dove that you might fly away and be at rest. But you must resist this normal, human desire. You must *stay* and *pray!* You must *stretch* yourself out and *strive* in prayer! You must maintain and assert yourself before God in prayer. You must do battle by placing your prayers into battle array. And you must pray, pray, pray! As has been noted, the worst mistake David's enemies ever made was driving David, God's servant, to prayer, evening, morning, and at noon!

And be assured, dear praying heart, that if a way of escape becomes necessary in your grievous situation, if the heat of battle becomes more than you can bear, God, who is faithful, promises that *He* will provide a way out (1 Corinthians 10:13). *He* will deliver you. *He* will come to your aid. *He* will rescue you. *He* will see to it! You can depend on *Him*.

And until God makes that determination, you are to stay put, to see the situation through (or should I say, to *pray* the situation through?). And what will happen when you call upon God? As David declared, "The LORD shall save me...and He shall hear my voice" (Psalm 55:16-17)!

Lesson #3—Believe that God will sustain you. David's confidence in God is powerful. Like a stonemason, he labors steadily on in prayer, never letting up, repeatedly hammering out his affirmations that God will sustain him: "The LORD shall save me....He shall hear my voice....God will hear, and afflict them...He shall never permit the righteous to be moved" (verses 16-22).

Finally, because of rehearsing over and over again all that God is and what He promises to do for His own, and because of continually feeding his broken heart with such truths, David shouts out his final assurance—"I will trust in You" (verse 23)! His prayers have at last broken through upon his own soul. At last, David dismisses his preoccupation with the enemy and turns his full focus—and trust—upon the Lord God Almighty who hears His people's pleas and saves them.

Oh, dear reading friend, when you are driven to distraction by the assaults of others, when you are wrestling with despair, when all seems hopeless, put your God-given faith to work and trust in the Lord. Believe it—in whatever burden you bear, He will sustain you today and all the days of your life!

Checklist for Prayer

✓ *Stay*—Stand firm against the desire to fly away, to leave, to try to avoid or escape your people-trials. Remember that "the wicked flee when no one pursues, but the righteous are bold as a lion" (Proverbs 28:1).

✓ *Pray*—Look up! When your soul is in sore straits, there is no solace and no cure comparable to prayer. That's exactly when you must seek God on bended knee. Resist, with God's help, the urge to emote. Refuse, with God's strength, to sink into a variety of emotional and/or sinful responses. Refrain, with God's self-control, from self-pity, self-righteousness, anger, and depression. Reject, with God's grace, the temptation to ask *Why*. Don't allow yourself to rant, rave, disintegrate into a puddle, fall apart, or collapse. Instead of fainting, pray (Luke 18:1)! And while you are praying, cast your cares and burdens upon the Lord (Psalm 55:22).

Every trial is both difficult and different. In fact, trials are manifold, various, and of every sort (James 1:2). Yet every trial, as difficult and different as it may be, is also common (1 Corinthians 10:13). Of course you may pray to bear your problems. However, you may need to share it. You may need to seek counsel and advice. God can and will use others to help bear your burdens (Galatians 6:2) and to advise you if it is time to leave your situation, if it is time to speak up instead of staying silent. Many times God's answers to your prayers are *people*—people He sends and uses to assist you and advise you, people who have been through the same kind of trial you are suffering, people who are wise.

And speaking of wisdom, here's some advice I received about hurtful situations. Don't let them spill over into your relationships with family or friends. And don't allow a root of bitterness to develop in your heart (Hebrews 12:15). Its bitter poison will infect you first and then spread to the lives of those closest to you. *You* will get over your suffering. *You* will go on. *You* may even forget about a painful incident...but will *they?* Will *others?*

So with God's help and with much prayer, go on with life, silently, cheerfully, in the power and grace of the Holy Spirit (Galatians 5:22-23), and with good advice (Proverbs 20:18). Go on in the confidence that God is still on His throne. He is still in control, He is still sovereign, He is still all-powerful, and He is still able...and He always will be! And He will...He *will*...judge the unrighteous and deal with those who harm His children (Psalm 37:6). He promises it!

✓   *Weigh*—Pay attention and look for the good that is coming from your trial. Your all-powerful God, who promises to work all things together for your good (Romans 8:28), will sweeten that which is bitter. And after all, where does humility grow? And trust? And faith? It grows in the crucible of the fire of trials... when there is no place else to turn or to look but upward into the face of your superintending God.

Beloved sufferer, every cloud has a silver lining, but you must look for it! God *is* blessing you. It's His nature. However, in the darkness of your pain you may have to search for it. So begin a page in your prayer notebook or journal called "Blessings Never to Be Forgotten." The psalmist advises us to "forget not all His benefits" (Psalm 103:2). Don't let even one of God's brilliant blessings go unnoticed! Capture it with your butterfly net—your pen!—and mount it on paper to be admired, remembered, and cherished for today, tomorrow, and for all time. Then you can give testimony to the goodness of the Lord...even in the midst of trials that are not so good.

Answering God's Call to You

Dear one, God is calling you to pray, in the bad times as well as the good. So remember to answer His call and pray during the bad times—to contend in prayer! And do remember to do as David did and pray passionately. David not only poured out his prayers, he pounded them out. In dire distress, "David prayed in *anguish* with respect to himself, in *anger* with respect to his enemies, and in *assurance* with respect to God."[4]

Pray passionately, but also pray often. Even though David couldn't fly away from his situation, his soul flew away to heaven in prayer. His prayers became like the wings of the dove he wished for, that ascended fast and quickly and went far toward heaven. And fly away they did…often! "Evening and morning and at noon I will pray, and cry aloud" (Psalm 55:17).

Pray regularly, too. It's obvious that David must have committed himself to a regular pattern of prayer during his crises. He took his issues to God in prayer at least three times a day, and so can—and should—you. Whatever your present aching trial, you must make the decision that David made: "As for me, I will call upon God, and the Lord shall save me" (verse 16).

And what will happen when you turn to God in prayer during your times of distress and pain? Your bitter ordeal will be sweetened. In your bad times—when your heart is hurting and your need for God's gentle touch is at its greatest and your heavy heart is the most sensitive—your prayers will be the most sweet and rewarding. Oh, please, don't wish these times away! Some of your most meaningful fellowships with God will come when you contend with Him over your hurting heart. So fly away in prayer…and rest in Him!

*The time we spend in solitude
with our heavenly Father and our Bible
is time spent waiting upon the Lord.
Afterward there is the mounting up,
the taking flight as an eagle.
We are able to soar because
we have been with the Lord.*

—ELIZABETH GEORGE

8

When You Are Worshiping...Pray!

All of God's people love to worship Him! It seems we just can't find enough ways to express our feelings and gratitude toward God. And references to worship are everywhere! For instance...

The songs and hymns we love to sing—called *worship* music—usually also contain the word "worship" in their titles—or at least in their lyrics. Books galore make reference to *worship* in their titles and subtitles. Television and radio ministries make liberal use of the term *worship* in their uplifting and inspiring program titles. And at church we have a *worship* service where we are assisted by *worship* teams, *worship* bands, and *worship* leaders...who follow an order of *worship*.

We love to worship in these wonderful ways, don't we? And yet there is another means by which you and I can worship God, and that is through the "sacrifice" of prayer.

The Sweet Aroma of Worship

Have you ever wondered about the tradition of *worship?* It has a thrilling and inspiring biblical history that showcases yet another facet in the gem of prayer.

Worship—In the Old Testament, much of the worship of God's people was related to the sacrificial system set down by God's law. Many of the offerings to God were burned, creating an upward-rising smoke and aroma. The sacrificial acts of the worshipers were associated with and accompanied by prayer, by the making of an entreaty to God. As the aroma of the sacrifices went up from the altar, prayers also ascended to God.

Incense—One of the specific offerings mandated by the law of God was the burning of incense. As you survey the list below, see for yourself how "sweet" the sacrificial offering of incense was. Then read on to witness two men who worshiped God through their prayers.

- Incense was a costly offering.

- Incense was a sign of the acknowledgment of deity.

- Incense produced an aromatic odor.

- Incense was known as the "sweet smoke."

- Incense could be burned only by priests.

- Incense was offered up only in "the holy place."

- Incense is used in the Bible as a symbol for prayer.

- Incense was offered up and burned every morning and evening along with the other daily morning and evening sacrifices.[1]

The Prayers of True Worshipers

The prayers of a king—King David was definitely a man who prayed and worshiped from the heart. The poetic, worshipful psalms he penned, prayed, and sang teach us much about prayer. In one particular psalm, David prayed to God with outstretched heart and hands, "Let my prayer be set before You as incense" (Psalm 141:2). David is referring to his prayer as being like the perfume that was burned on the altar of incense during worship in the tabernacle.

And note this important fact: This prayer of David's was not a hasty, spontaneous, impulsive outburst of worship and emotion. There is certainly a place for such impromptu prayer in our lives, but here David mentioned his prayer in a different light—it was "set before" God. He was pleading with God that his prayers would be as *disciplined* and *regular* as the offering of incense and burnt offerings were required to be according to God's law (Exodus 29:38–30:9).[2]

The prayers of a priest—Another man's experience with worship suggests the concept of worship being accompanied by prayer. His name was Zacharias, and he was the husband of Elizabeth (Luke 1:5-7). Zacharias was also a priest. And when it was time for his division of priests to perform their temple duties, Zacharias' "lot fell to burn *incense*" in the temple of the Lord (verses 8-9). As he went into the temple of the Lord to burn incense before the Lord, "the whole multitude of the people was *praying* outside at the hour of incense" (verse 10).

What a high honor! Because of the large number of priests, most of them would never be chosen to burn the incense...and not one of them was permitted to serve in this capacity twice.[3] In other words, to burn the incense during worship was a once-in-a-lifetime honor...that is, *if* the honor ever came your way!

And what did Zacharias do while he was inside the temple, in front of the very veil that divided the Holy Place from the Most Holy Place? (And what would you do if you were that "close" to God?) Zacharias prayed!

Again, we must realize that this is no chance happening. The burning of incense was a defined part of the organized worship of God as set down by God Himself (Exodus 30:7-8). And the incense was offered every morning and every night, as ordered by God. And everyone else, priests and people alike, stood outside the Holy Place...praying.

Dear reading friend, this is the way it went with the burning of the incense. It was a prescribed and formal part of the worship of God. It was set down as law. It consisted of ordered, orderly, and organized worship and prayer.

Furthermore, there was a specific *place* and *method* for offering the sweet aroma of incense and its accompanying prayers before God. And there was a specific *time* to offer them up. (There was even an exact *recipe* for making up the perfumed incense—Exodus 30:34-35!) This form of worship was not left to chance, to impulse, to human creativity, fancy, and feelings. No, God dictated it.

Now...back to Zacharias. Prayer went up to God any time a sacrifice was made or incense was burned and the smoke of the sacrifice went up. And what happened to Zacharias? "Then an angel of the Lord appeared to him, standing on the right side of the altar of incense." And the angel said, "Your prayer is heard" (Luke 1:11,13).

Did you catch all of this? Here is a priest...whose lot fell to go into the temple to offer worship, who is burning incense and praying. And the people are praying while the incense is being burned. And Zacharias' prayer was heard!

The prayers of your heart—As New Testament worshipers, you and I don't kill and burn animals or incense as a sacrifice to the Lord. But, dear one, we as women after God's own heart are called to offer up a different kind of sacrifice—that of prayer. We are to lift our prayers to the Lord. We are to offer the "incense" of our prayers. And as you and I both know, that calls for some sacrifice on our part! What kind? As you work your way through the following list of "sacrifices," use it as a personal checklist.

ℰhecklist for 𝒫rayer

✓   *Sacrifice your carelessness*—Lax attitudes toward God and toward prayer have to go. We must substitute "I'll get around to it...I'll pray later...I'll pray when I feel like it...I'll pray when it's convenient for me...Catch You next time, Lord!" with a sober-mindedness about what prayer is and to do it with greater planning and more careful preparation. David *ordered* his prayers, precisely laying them out. And Zacharias prayed at a certain time and in a most reverent and mindful way—in worship!

Be sure you pray as often as you please. No Christian should be able to take a single breath of air without making that breath a prayer! But also set a *time* to pray—your time! Pick a *place* to pray—your place! And have a *plan* for prayer—your prayer notebook! These three decisions will assist your heart in offering up your prayers to God. Are all three an established part of your prayer-life today?

✓ *Sacrifice your sin*—Do you desire to pray powerfully and effectively? Such prayer requires that we deal seriously with our sin. God's standard for our prayers is clear: "If I regard iniquity in my heart, the Lord will not hear" (Psalm 66:18). "The LORD is far from the wicked, but He hears the prayer of the righteous" (Proverbs 15:29). "One who turns away his ear from hearing the law, even his prayer is an abomination" (Proverbs 28:9). "The eyes of the LORD are on the righteous, and His ears are open to their prayers" (1 Peter 3:12).

As believers in Christ who enjoy "new" life in Him, we are called to "put off" and "put away" the sins that were a part of our "old" life—our life before Christ (Ephesians 4:22-32 and Colossians 3:5-14). We are to sacrifice our favorite sins—to put them away, give them up, get rid of them. Can you think of any leftover behaviors from your former life? If so, identify, name, and confess them. Then put them off and put them away. God will delight in helping you eradicate them!

✓ *Sacrifice your heart*—Prayer involves the offering of your emotions and tears. It's a terrible, ugly thing, but when we don't pray, it's easy to become aloof, controlled, cool, and distant. We are unattached, untouched, and uncaring about what is happening around us and about the pain in people's hearts. But when we make the decision to pray, it costs us our hearts. The only way I can describe it is to say that the act of prayer breaks our hearts. Then...*then!*...our emotions spill over and our tears flow. We are burning the "incense" of our sincere prayers toward the Lord, offering up the sacrifice of our hearts. Scripture tells that "the sacrifices" God is interested in "are a broken spirit, a broken and a contrite heart"—a crushed heart (Psalm 51:17). Does this describe your heart?

Here's a prayer suggestion. When you pray tomorrow, make it a point to ask nothing for yourself. Of course you'll want to deal with any sin and take care of your "account" with God. But ask nothing for yourself. Instead, spend the precious sacrifice of your prayer time praying for others. And go ahead—spend some of your tears, too!

Answering God's Call to You

Dear seeker of God's heart, I know you, like me, desire the sweet aroma of worship and prayer to envelop you, to radiate from your very being, to scent all that you touch and do. I also know that you, as a woman of God, wish to answer His call to be a devoted pray-er and worshiper. So whether you are a seasoned prayer-warrior who aspires to continue in the battle or a prayer "wanna-be" who wonders how to take that first step toward communing with "the Eternal," you must—absolutely must!—take the sacred start-up step that follows. Although it is listed last in our chapter, it's unquestionably first...and must be first each and every day of your God-given life.

✓ *Sacrifice your time*—Number One on my list of sacrifices is time because that's the thing I never seem to have enough of! You and I have many witnesses throughout history who offered up the sacrifice of their time so they could offer up the sacrifice of their prayers and worship. For instance....

—John Wesley, busy founder of Methodism, spent at least two hours each day in prayer. He is famous for bringing us these challenging words: "I have so much to do that I must spend several hours in prayer before I am able to do it."

—Samuel Rutherford, seventeenth-century theologian, rose at three o'clock each morning to "wait upon God."

—Alexander MacLaren, English clergyman and scholar, wrote that he owed his "success" to the habit never broken of spending one hour a day alone with the Eternal. It was this man, who knew well the sweet savor of the perfume of prayers of worship, who wrote, "The garments of those who pray smell of all the fragrances that grow about the feet of the King."[4]

—And Martin Luther, German Reformer, testified, "Prayer is the most important thing in my life. If I should neglect prayer for a single day, I should lose a great deal of the fire of my faith."[5]

Prayer is sweet worship. But it's also true that prayer is spiritual *work!* And it's always difficult to get to our work, isn't it? But we simply must realize that *every*thing—all our best work and good deeds—hinges upon our offering up the sacrifice of a portion of our precious, hard-to-come-by, scarce, limited time.

Do you have a lot to do today? Then by all means offer up the sacrifice of your time...and pray! Do you have chores to do that you think absolutely cannot wait? Then be sure you pay tribute to God and take time to wait on the Lord...in prayer. Do you desire to partake of the perfumed smell of all the fragrances that grow about the feet of the King? Then spend a handful of your golden minutes. Spread them at the feet of your Lord, kneel low...and pray! Do you desire more fire in your faith? Then to gain the unmeasurable heat of great faith, give to God a measure of your time...and pray. Answer God's call to you. O worship the King...and pray!

The way to worry about nothing
is to pray about everything.[1]

When You Are
Worried...Pray!

Would you like to meet a first-class worrywart? Well, check that off your goal list. You have ...and it's me! In fact, I should write a book entitled *Confessions of a Worrywart*. But until then, suffice it to say that I've seen the inside of a doctor's office more than a few times for such maladies as a bleeding ulcer, colitis, and eczema covering my hands and arms up to my elbows. And I know I'm not alone! Women love to worry...about anything and everything. We worry about our health along with our husbands' and parents' health.

On the heels of health concerns comes anguish over relationships. If a woman is married, she worries about her relationship with her husband, followed by worries about being a good mom. And if she's not married, she worries about that—about *Why?* and *What if...?*

And we've all got family...so *voila!*...here's yet another area for stewing. We worry about family relationships.

Then we move right on down the list and extend our fretting to relationships with friends and acquaintances. And we can't stop there! Oh no, we've also got to worry about relationships and difficulties with our enemies—about knowing what to do and how to handle these problems!

Once any children are raised, the worries continue to be pumped out to now include agonizing about our grown children, their marriages, moving right along to include the next generation in our worries as we transfer our anxieties to our grandchildren.

And what about jobs and careers? My Jim and I were in Manhattan the day of the September 11, 2001, World Trade Center tragedy. As we've followed up on the continuing effects of that disaster on New Yorkers, we still hear that many continue to worry not only about another terrorist attack, but also about keeping a job or losing the job they have, while others have never found a job since their workplace or their company's economy was destroyed as a repercussion of the Trade Center collapse. Unfortunately such job problems are common in all 50 states, causing worry everywhere.

Then there are other entries on "The Great List of Things to Worry About" that include worrying about what others think of us, worrying about safety, finances, the future, nicely topped off with worrying about aging, worrying about getting up in front of others whether on the job or in a ministry, worrying about getting the house ready for company or an upcoming social event. On and on our worry lists and tendencies stretch. And yet…

God Commands, "Do Not Worry!"

Did you know that over 300 times in the New Testament God commands us, "Do not worry" or "Be not anxious"? Just one of these occurrences, which we considered earlier, is Philippians 4:6-7:

> Be anxious for nothing, but in everything by prayer and supplication, with thanksgiving, let your requests be made known to God; and the peace of God, which surpasses all understanding, will guard your hearts and minds through Christ Jesus.

Beloved, these are the verses that knocked some sense into me about my worrying habit and its devastating effects. After I wrote out this golden key to peace of mind and memorized it, and as I reviewed it and recited it over and over, carried it with me, and took it apart word-by-word, it began to transform my heart and mind. I went from worrying to worshiping. Instead of fretting, I began to trust the God of the promise. Here's what I discovered.

The command—"Be anxious for nothing." God's Word is clear in instructing us to take care of our responsibilities and families and to carefully manage all that we possess. But beyond that, the Bible is also crystal clear in letting us know that we are *not* to worry...about anything...ever...period!

In the book of Philippians, where this gem for worriers is found, we witness many causes for worry. First of all, the Philippians themselves had problems with their enemies in their battle for the faith of the gospel (Philippians 1:27-28), which threatened their joy in the Lord (3:1) and their strength for the battle (4:1). Then there was Paul, the man who is writing this exhortation. Talk about problems! Paul was in prison...waiting to see if he would live or die! On top of his stressful situation, Paul also suffered from some kind of physical or personal "thorn in the flesh" (2 Corinthians 12:7).

Writing from his own problem-afflicted life, Paul shared this command with his friends in Philippi...and with you and me: "Be anxious for nothing." These four words, breathed from the heart of God through His servant Paul, make it plain to see that, for the Christian, all worry is forbidden by God.

The scope of the command—"Be anxious *for nothing.*" I once heard a Bible teacher ask, "Do you know what 'nothing' is? It's a zero with the rim kicked off!" Well, dear one, that's God's message to our hearts. When it comes to worrying, we are to be anxious *for nothing.* Or, as one Greek scholar translates it, "Stop being anxious about any-thing."[2] In the words of another Bible translation, "Do not worry about anything."[3] There aren't many other words beyond *nothing* and *anything* to use to describe the scope of God's command!

Are you wondering, Yes, I see it...but how? Well, take heart! God anticipated your desire to stop worrying and your need to escape the physical, emotional, and mental toll worry takes on our lives. Here's God's answer to all your problems—

The solution—Prayer! *"Let your requests be made known to God."* Yes, life is difficult, problem-ridden, and filled with stress. And yes, worry is a natural tendency. And praise God, yes, there is something we can do to keep from worrying! And yes, we *can* obey God's command to *"be anxious for nothing."* God's solution is: When you are worried...pray! Pray from your heart and with all your heart! Pray, pray, pray!

And like the colors in the swath of a rainbow across the sky, God gives us several brilliant avenues for triumphing over worry. Instead of worrying about anything, He says, *"in everything...let your requests be made known to God."* How?

🐾   By prayer—Prayer is not only worship but prayer is where all true worship begins...and all worry ends!

🐾   By supplication—Do you have a need? (Or, more accurately asked, Do you *think* you have a need?) Then pray! Petition God by supplication. Boldly go before His throne of grace in your times of need... and with your needs (Hebrews 4:16). Don't fail to shoot your prayers heavenward and ask the all-powerful, Almighty God of the universe—the only One who can solve your problems! Doing so is His remedy for worry. We can ask and not worry...or we can worry because we don't ask. It's one or the other—and the choice is ours.

🐾   With thanksgiving—Praise, gratitude, and thanksgiving accompany all true prayer. A thankful heart that focuses on the fact that all difficulties are within God's sovereign purposes cannot be a worrying heart. Neither can a heart of trust, a heart that is at rest, a heart that knows that God causes all things to work together for good (Romans 8:28-29). Oh, give Him thanks!

🐾   By requests—Present your requests to God with utmost confidence. Keep nothing back, neither great nor small. Withhold nothing—none of your concerns—from God. He wants your *every*thing, your every concern! So present them to Him. Leave them in the lap of the Almighty.

The result—When you and I are obedient to God's command to not worry, and when we're faithful to pray instead, *the peace of God* comes to our rescue and "will guard [our] hearts and minds through Christ Jesus." In other words, as a tribal missionary so beautifully and simply translated this truth, *Jesus will make your heart sit down.*

And once your heart sits down, peace keeps watch over it. Like a soldier, God's peace guards your heart—and mind!—against anxiety, doubt, fear, worry, and distress. And the result? The battle against worry is won!

Checklist for Prayer

✓ *Don't...*miss a day of prayer—If you play hit-and-miss with your daily prayer time, you will most certainly discover that your worry level is higher on the days when you don't pray. Prayer is God's surefire solution for eliminating worry. *If* you pray, *then* you won't be anxious. *If* you pray, *then* you will experience peace of mind. And the opposite is true, too. *If* you don't pray, *then* you will be anxious. *If* you don't pray, *then* you will not experience peace of mind.

So be faithful to pray. Be faithful to write down the issues that tempt you to worry and address them in prayer. And be wise to realize that anything is sufficient to cause anxiety if it is not prayed about!

Also be faithful to memorize Scripture. It's a weapon in your arsenal to be used every day as you do battle against worrying. If you don't know which scriptures...

✓ *Do...*memorize Psalm 23—You're probably already familiar with this well-loved psalm, but put it to memory. When my husband resigned from his well-paying job, with about every benefit a human being would ever need, to enter seminary as a student who just happened to have a wife and two pre-schoolers(!), my worries hit an all-time high.

It was then that I memorized "The Shepherd Psalm." I wrote it out on six 3" x 5" cards, putting one verse on each card. And I carried these cards with me everywhere I went. If I was driving, I was memorizing and reciting. If I was walking, I was memorizing and reciting. If I was showering, I was memorizing and reciting. If I was sitting in a room waiting...for a doctor's appointment, for Bible study to begin, for choir practice to start, I was memorizing and reciting. And, of course, if I was standing in a line waiting, I was memorizing and reciting.

Two things happened. First, my worries decreased because I was immersed in these sacred truths about God's character and His care for His own. And second, when I did worry, I almost automatically went back to the 12 powerful life-changing, worry-reducing, promises contained in Psalm 23.

Well, I don't have to tell you that due to God's care for us, Jim and I and our two girls made it through those financially challenging hard times of change. This "pearl of the psalms" served me well through those trying days...and all that have followed in their wake. Because it is so ingrained in my daily life and thought process, an added blessing has been the many opportunities I've had to share it with other worriers through teaching and writing about its instructive truths.[4]

✓ *Do...*determine a "worry day"—I can't resist passing on this fun—and funny!—practical solution for those times you think you just have to have some measure of worry in your emotional diet.

A man who was unable to put his troubles aside completely decided that the next best thing to do would be to set apart a single day, Wednesday, to do all his worrying. When something came up that disturbed him during the week, he wrote it down and put it in what he called his "Wednesday Worry Box."

When the time came to review his high-anxiety problems, he found to his great surprise that most of them had already been settled and no longer generated anxiety! He discovered that most worry is unnecessary and a waste of precious energy.[5]

Answering God's Call to You

My faithful reading friend, worry is real...and God knows that. Therefore, He addresses it throughout Scripture and faithfully instructs you in exactly what you must do—and not do—and why.

For instance, when Jesus' disciples expressed their worries and concerns, Jesus did not chastise them, put them down, belittle them, or give them a spiritual spanking. No, he sat down with them and talked about it, straightforwardly, specifically, and understandingly. And He told them exactly what to do—and not do—and why.

Are you curious about His advice? He told them, "*Do not worry* about tomorrow, for tomorrow will worry about its own things. Sufficient for the day is its own trouble" (Matthew 6:34).

Beloved, this is still how God deals with you and your worries today. And His advice to the disciples applies to you, too, as a solution for your worries today. And guess what? His advice to the disciples will still apply to you as a solution for your worries...tomorrow.

As we leave this all-too-familiar—and worrisome!—subject, I want you to take away these two truths. First, realize that you will become worried, anxious, and fearful when you *fail to trust* in God's wisdom, power, and goodness. Prayer dispels your fear that God may not be wise enough, strong enough, or good enough to prevent disaster. God has an amazing storehouse from which He is able to draw all that is necessary to take care of you, His child. He has—and gives to you...

> "The riches of His grace" (Ephesians 1:7),
>   an inexhaustible reservoir to draw from.
> "The riches of His glory" (Ephesians 3:16),
>   an inestimable wealth to count on.
> "The riches of His goodness" (Romans 2:4),
>   an unfailing resource to rely on.

Second, realize that the means to answering God's call to not worry is entwined with His call to pray. Therefore, do not *fail to pray*. When you are anxious and choose to answer your call to pray instead of worry, God answers your prayers as you call to Him. Prayer sets you free from fear and worry. Therefore, when you are worried...pray!

$\mathscr{S}$ide $\mathscr{E}$ffects...

Self-Doubt

It is a downward spiral that focuses on the negative and why things cannot be done versus why things can be done. It is a sinkhole, a debilitating attitude, and a terrible habit.

Mediocrity

Capable people who worry are rendered incapable of accomplishing their intended goal. Worry makes you peck around on the ground like a chicken when you were intended to soar like an eagle.

Fright

People who worry are not being cautious or thinking things over; they are simply scared. Running scared is the enemy of success, peace, contentment, happiness, joy, laughter, etc.

No Spark

The excitement is gone. Worry lets the air out of all you do, draining the fun and excitement from everything.

No Creativity

The freedom to be creative is squelched by worry. You simply cannot excel to your potential when worry controls your thoughts.

...of Worrying

Improper Shaping

You are molded and shaped by your thinking, and worries should not shape your future.

Hazy Results

Those who worry are second-guessing themselves, which produces a hesitancy that brings with it an unclear focus. Such a hazy goal will produce a hazy result.

Bad Habits

Worrying is a habit, the result of preconditioning and years of practice. The destructive habit of worrying turns people into prisoners.

Physical Ailments

The body reacts adversely to internal worries. John Haggai insightfully stated, "A distraught mind inevitably leads to a deteriorated body."

Wasted Time

Over 90 percent of what you worry about never comes to pass. To worry is to waste time; therefore, the more you worry, the less you accomplish.[6]

> *One groan,*
> *one sigh from a wounded soul,*
> *excels and prevails with God.*
>
> —WILLIAM PENN

10

When You Are Overwhelmed...Pray!

I'm sure you've been shaken to the core at some time in your life by a serious, earth-shattering, life-wrenching, seemingly overwhelming crisis. A time when you felt devastated. A time when you believed you could not go on...or weren't sure how to go on. Unfortunately, pain and sorrow, loss and tragedy, confusion and frustration touch every life. It's terrible, isn't it?

If numbing trials are a fact of life, the question then becomes, What can I do when my life is enveloped in such experiences? And the answer? You (and I!) can immediately go to God because He has a set of instructions for making life work when it seems like it will never work again. God has given you two magnificent resources for managing a crushing situation.

First, when you are overwhelmed, you have the Bible, which is God's guidebook for dealing with all of life and its every challenge (2 Peter 1:3). And second...

Trust in God's Help with Prayer

You and I can thank our Lord that through the act of prayer we can seek the heart and mind of God *in* our difficult situations. By yet another facet in the mysterious and magnificent gem of prayer, God gives us help for tending to our lives...and for answering His call to prayer. He gives us this assurance for our difficult times:

> Likewise the Spirit also helps in our weaknesses. For we do not know what we should pray for as we ought, but the Spirit Himself makes intercession for us with groanings which cannot be uttered....He makes intercession for the saints according to the will of God (Romans 8:26-27).

In picturesque words we discover that God Himself gives us help...and hope! The Holy Spirit literally comes to our "rescue" as He "happens" upon us in our trouble. He ministers to us by lending His helping hand in pleading and interceding to God in our behalf, with groans and "sighs that baffle words."[1] In simple language, He groans and sighs for us in prayer.

What good news! When you or I don't know what to pray for, how to pray, or what words to use, the Holy Spirit does! And He takes over and expresses our requests *for* us. He intercedes for us by appealing to the only Person who can help us—God Himself. The Spirit's "groaning" or "sighing" in prayer to God the Father for us becomes effective intercession on our behalf. One Bible scholar went so far as to refer to such "grim struggling" in prayer as "Gethsemane groans."[2]

Yes, we can definitely thank God that we are not left to our own resources to cope with our problems.

A Personal Word of Testimony

A red-letter day—On a particular Monday several years ago, I experienced being overwhelmed in a personal way. On that day I tasted what it feels like to not be able to pray...to not even know how to pray. Yet at the same time, I knew that I desperately needed to pray!

I was sitting at home at my desk working on a message for the women's Bible study I was scheduled to teach on Wednesday. I'd done it scores of times as a Bible teacher, but on that day I was having a terrible time. I could not think. I could not focus. I could not settle down. Why? Because that red-letter day was the very morning my mother was scheduled to be checked into a nursing home. Two of my brothers were there in my growing-up town in Oklahoma, present to assist my 93-year-old father with this most difficult task and transition. Despite the distance between California and Oklahoma, my brothers and I were in constant contact until they bundled up my beloved mother to head for the nursing home.

Overwhelmed by emotions—And what was I feeling? First of all, I felt guilty because I wasn't there with my family. Yet I knew full well that God had sovereignly arranged my schedule so there was no way that I could be present for that milestone occasion. So there I sat, at home, alone, some 1,500 miles away. I was absolutely helpless as my little 87-year-old mother was being moved to a care facility. Due to osteoporosis, she was all of four-and-a-half-feet tall, and, due to Alzheimer's, she was at the mentality of about a two-year-old. It also didn't help to recall that my parents had been married 67 years and that my dad would now live alone in the house he and my mother had shared for more than 40 years.

So there I was at home...with an over-active imagination...envisioning all of this process happening, all that would be involved in it, all of my little mother's feelings and my dad's feelings.

And then, of course, I was trying to deal with *my* anguish! Needless to say, it was a really rough day. Finally I got to the point where I just put my head down and sobbed. I couldn't pray! I couldn't pray for my mother. I couldn't pray for my dad. I couldn't pray for my brothers. I couldn't even pray for myself. All I could do was silently sob and pour out what the church father Augustine referred to as "liquid prayers."

God's grace to me—Oh, was it ever an agonizing day! When Jim came home from work that evening, we talked about what a personally strenuous and emotional day it had been. At last I said, "I know I should call my dad," and then I added, "but I just don't think I can."

"But, Liz, you've got to," said my all-wise Jim, who reached over, picked up the phone, dialed the number, and then turned and handed the phone to me.

Sure enough, my dad answered the phone...and he was as cheerful as cheerful can be! He said, "Hi there, Elizabeth Ann, would you like to speak to your mother? She's sitting right here!"

As my dad explained after a joyous (on my part) "talk" with my mom (who was oblivious to all that was happening), the doctor had not been able to sign the papers that day, and my dear sweet mother was still at home, right where she'd been all my life, on the loveseat in the family room, snuggled right next to my dad.

I have to report to you that I believe to this day that unsigned form and my dad's cheer and my mother's voice was the Lord's grace to me. I thank *Him* that I was able to talk to her just one more time sitting comfortably on the sofa beside my dad in her home. It was truly a tender, personal gift from God to me, His suffering child.

The end of the story—My mom went into the nursing home the next day, never to come out again until her death six years later. But for me, in that time on that Monday, something—perhaps everything—got settled with the Lord as I sought the words to tell Him all about my broken heart...and found none.

That's the way it is for us when we are in sorrow or affliction, when we are suffering from physical or emotional distress, when we must pray for our children—or our parents!—or our loved ones with such sorrowful hearts that we don't even know how to pray or what to say to God. Even women with a lifetime of prayer under their belts run up against such heart-breaking sorrow and prayer-robbing experiences.

A word for you—Again I say to you, "Thank God!" Thank Him that He knows your weaknesses, that He knows your heart, that He knows your suffering, that He knows your desire and your need to pray. He also knows when you cannot pray, so *He*, through His Holy Spirit, comes to your rescue and prays for you! Thank Him that He has so graciously allowed this avenue of prayer, this whisper, this sigh, this groan of prayer by the Spirit, for those times when words and understanding fail you. You can pour out the contents of your broken, confused heart as best you can, *if* you can(!)…and leave the rest of your efforts to communicate with God to the power and ability of the Holy Spirit.

Now, what exactly can—and should—you do when you run up against an overwhelming adversity?

Checklist for Prayer

✓ *Do your best*—Sometimes your heart cries out, "It hurts so much! It's so bad I don't think I can pray!" What are you to do when this happens? First, remember such feelings are okay! They are normal. They are *common* (1 Corinthians 10:13). This happens to everyone. This is not an indictment against your spirituality. You haven't failed.

But be sure you do your best to pray. At least assume the posture of prayer. Go ahead and attempt to pray. Pray in the ways that you do know about how to pray…adoring and worshiping God for who He is and what He has done for you and His people, thanking God for His goodness, acknowledging any known sin, praying for others.

Just begin. That's your part. God's part is to "join in and help" you pray.[3] He will perfect your fumbling attempts to do the right thing—to pray even when your heart hurts so badly that you are not sure what to pray or how to pray. He will intercede and groan for you. As explained by a Greek scholar, "The Holy Spirit lays hold of our weaknesses along with us and carries his part of the burden facing us as if we were carrying a log, one at each end."[4]

✓   *Try to pray*—At other times, we throw our hands up, turn our heads and hearts up to heaven, and say to God, "I don't know what to pray!" Once again, remember this too is okay. It's normal. It's common. It happens to everyone. Again, your confusion and inability are not indictments against your spirituality. You haven't failed.

But the solution is also the same! Just pray...or try to pray. Assume the posture of prayer. Go ahead and attempt to pray. Go through the beginning motions—your familiar words and practices for your periods of prayer in better times.

Try! That's your job, your role. Then, as you turn to Him and attempt to pray from your heart, God will lead you. He will guide you. His Holy Spirit will even do the praying for you.

✓   *Watch your heart*—Don't worry about your words. It's your heart that counts! In prayer, we can be quite eloquent in language, pray memorized Scripture verses, borrow phrases and verbiage from the prayers of old and the people we admire. We can pontificate and strut our education, emote, cause our voice to tremor, even cry. Or, in the case of the overwhelmed heart, we are speechless.

But God is not as interested in your words as He is in your heart! Man looks—and hears—on the outside, but God looks at—and hears—the heart (1 Samuel 16:7). And in a parable, Jesus praised the blunt, agonized prayer of the tax collector over that of the eloquent boasting of a knowledgeable religious leader. As Jesus pointed out, the Pharisee, for all his words, "prayed with himself" but the repentant's prayer was heard (Luke 18:9-14).

The psalmist wrote a prayer of his own that we should remember: "Let...the meditation of my heart be acceptable in Your sight, O LORD" (Psalm 19:14). In prayer it's easier to get the words right than it is to get the heart right.

Answering God's Call to You

God is so good! And He is all-knowing. He has anticipated our every need, even our need—and inability!—to pray in the midst of crippling physical, emotional, or spiritual distress. For those difficult times, God has provided the companionship of the Holy Spirit. God makes it possible to answer His call to prayer even in our weakness, to make our desire to pray—even when overwhelmed—a reality.

How encouraging it is to know that, as believers, we are not left to our own resources to cope with life's difficulties and problems. Even when we don't know the right words to pray, the Holy Spirit prays with us and for us. And God answers! That means that with God helping us pray, we don't need to be afraid to come before him. We simply trust the Holy Spirit to intercede for us "in accordance with God's will" (Romans 8:27 NIV). We do our best to bring our requests to God, trusting that He will always do what is best.

And there's more! Consider these encouraging words from Romans, chapter 8:

—The Holy Spirit intercedes *for you* (verse 26).
—God is *for you* (verse 31).
—Christ makes intercession *for you* (verse 34).

What incredible, divine resources are yours, dear struggling friend! The Godhead is at work on your behalf. The Trinity watches over your welfare. God's eye is on the sparrow (Matthew 10:29-31) ...and He watches over you, too. Not a hair of your head falls to the ground that God does not know about it (Luke 12:7)...and neither does one of your sincere, heartfelt prayers, even one of your sincere, heartfelt *attempts* at prayer! Even your tears—your "liquid prayers"—are precious to your attentive Father, for He stores them in His bottle (Psalm 56:8).

So my prayer for you at this moment is that you will let the prayers of your heart flow! When you are in pain...pray! When you are speechless... pray! When you are heartsick...pray! When you are suffering, beaten up, or beaten down by life...pray! When you are troubled or perplexed... pray! When you are overwhelmed...pray! Your heavenly Father knows what you have need of before you ask (Matthew 6:32)...so ask. Use any fumbling words or wails you can muster up out of your hurting heart. Just be sure you pray...and leave the rest to God.

Just like a plant with its roots
hidden underground, you and I—
out of public view and alone with God—
are to draw from Him all that we need
to live the abundant life
He has promised His children.

—ELIZABETH GEORGE

When You Are in Need...Pray!

Like you, I enjoy praying. Yet I do admit that prayer is work. Each round of prayer requires a decision, determination, and discipline before our requests get off the ground. To shoot our prayers heavenward takes strength, aim, skill, and will. But I've noticed that I can easily fall into the habit of asking routinely, "God, please bless this, please bless that, please bless me, and please bless everyone!" Such automatic roteness in prayer reminds me of the shorthand a stenographer hurriedly scrawls out when trying to quickly write down dictated matter. With shorthand, you write as fast and as briefly as you can, taking every shortcut possible without losing the gist of the spoken material. The goal? Just get it down!

But then there is an author, who labors meticulously at the craft of writing. With writing, you do just that. You write. You begin the process of creating and polishing. Next there is the re-writing and re-polishing, which is followed by re-vising, re-re-writing(!), re-re-polishing(!), finishing, spit-shining, and signing off on first a sentence, then a paragraph, a page, a chapter...until finally, one or two thousand hours later, there's a book!

Believe me, there is a vast difference in these two forms of "writing." I know because I just happen to be a qualified, certified, credentialed, and seasoned teacher of shorthand ...and I just happen to be an author. And I can also tell you from experience that the sloppy, brief, hurried, and heartless flinging of our "God-bless" prayers up to God is like shorthand, while laboring for weeks, months, and years in intense prayer for a personal and specific ongoing need is like the painstaking art of writing....

Which brings me to you and your call to prayer!

I'm sure you're like me—you have a long list of needs. As we've already established in this book, we encounter trouble daily. We get hurt by others. We can become overwhelmed by the trials and tribulations of life. Plus we have our doubts, our worries, and our own set of reasons for not being as faithful as we'd like to be when it comes to the spiritual discipline of prayer.

So what can we do?

The next facet sculpted into God's jewel of prayer provides instruction regarding the personal needs of our hearts and lives as women—

Make Your Needs Known to God

The Bible speaks of making our requests known to God. We are instructed "in everything by prayer and *supplication*, with thanksgiving, let your requests be made known to God" (Philippians 4:6). We are told to be "praying always with all prayer and *supplication* in the Spirit" (Ephesians 6:18).

While the word "prayer" is a general term for worshipful conversation with God, *supplication* or *petition* (NIV), as we learned in Chapter 5, refers to a prayer with a sense of need. In other words, there is something you can—and should!—do about the pressing needs in your life, your family, your marriage, your friendships, your schooling, your job, and your everyday life: You are to petition God in supplication about your *specific* needs—to pray *specifically* concerning the issues in your life. For instance,

> Isaac prayed for his wife Rebekah to conceive (Genesis 25:21).
>
> Leah prayed to conceive (Genesis 30:17).
>
> Rebekah prayed to conceive (Genesis 30:22).
>
> Hannah prayed for a son (1 Samuel 1:11).
>
> Zacharias prayed for a child (Luke 1:13).
>
> Paul prayed for the salvation of his countrymen, for the Philippians, and for Timothy.
>
> Jesus prayed about His death (Matthew 26:36-46).

Our Savior and these saints of old prayed for specific needs, desires, and requests. And we are to do the same. We must lift up the particulars and the personal needs in our lives to God through specific supplications and petitions.

Praying About Your Personal Needs

If your life is anything like mine, tops on your list of personal needs is...

Health and energy—God has given us hefty job-assignments as Christian women. Our to-do lists are long...and so are our days! A multitude of people depend on us. And we need stamina, endurance, vitality, a God-perspective, purposeful focus, and staying power to continue reaching forward and pressing toward the goal of getting our work done (Philippians 3:13-14).

Attitude—Also on my personal prayer list is a joyful spirit, patience with any obstacles...or people-problems!...that come up along the way through my day, and self-control in speech so emotions don't spill out and hurt someone else (Galatians 5:22-23).

Faithfulness—I also pray to keep my eye—and heart!—fixed on the end of the day so that I will, Lord willing, continue pressing and reaching to its end. I pray to finish fully on my projects, whether that is finishing a chapter, running one last errand when I would dearly love to skip it and go on home, cleaning up the kitchen, dealing with trash, and tidying up the house last thing at night, even though I'm dog-tired and am tempted to say, "I'll deal with it first thing in the morning." I pray to be "faithful in all things" (1 Timothy 3:11).

Finances—And how about finances? That's something else I pray about every day—to hold up my end of the finances...like holding down the spending, paying any bills that are due (and remembering to record the payments in my checkbook!), and cultivating a generous heart (Proverbs 31:20).

Work—My "work" may be different than yours, but if you have a job, then your supplications should include your work environment, your faithfulness on the job, and the wise financial management of your paycheck. Pray from your heart to work willingly with your heart and hands..."as to the Lord" (Proverbs 31:13 and Colossians 3:23).

Wisdom—And every woman needs God's wisdom with decision making! So we must be about the business of petitioning God in supplication and asking for it: "If any of you lacks wisdom, let him ask of God...and it will be given to him" (James 1:5).

Relationships—Every woman also has relationships with parents and family members that need to be prayed over, not to mention her friends and her desire for companionship, camaraderie, and fellowship with wise people (1 Corinthians 15:33). Indeed, prayer perfumes every relationship! We must pray, too, to do our part in the Family and Public Relations Department and, "as much as depends on [us], live peaceably with all men" (Romans 12:18).

Again, what can we do with and about the concerns of our daily lives? *Pray!* "In everything by prayer and *supplication*, with thanksgiving, let your requests be made known to God."

Praying About Your Needs as a Married Woman

Are you married? Then which of the following is your Number One need in the Wife Department? "Lord, I need You to work in my husband's life—to help him find a job, to cause him to desire to grow in the Lord, to encourage him to be the leader in our marriage, to move him to be more involved as a father, to prompt him to take a more active role in disciplining the children, to create a hunger and thirst in him to want to go to church, to save his soul."

The Bible instructs that if your husband is not a Christian, you can send a loud and clear message for Christ to your spouse "without a word" (1 Peter 3:1)! But, dear sweet pray-er, you can surely be sending up your heart-cries to

God every day and every minute of every day as you pray, minute-by-minute, step-by-step, and word-by-word.

So what can a married woman do with and about the concerns of her daily needs as a wife and for her particular husband, her individual marital situation? Remember, God promises to supply all your needs (Philippians 4:19), so *pray!* Ask Him to work in your marriage.

Praying About Your Personal Needs as a Mother

I once read a book entitled *The Joys and Sorrows of Motherhood*. And, believe me, every mother knows that these two extreme emotions are an almost daily reality! So, precious mom, which of these pleas reflects your needs in this most emotional of all roles, that of mothering your children, stepchildren, or grandchildren? "Lord, I need you to work in my children's lives...to cause them to embrace the Christian faith, to move them to seek to grow spiritually, to work in their hearts to desire Christian friends and boyfriends or girlfriends, to impress upon them to want to marry a Christian mate."

And, as time passes, your prayer-needs and requests for your children graduate, too, as you begin praying for them to mature, find jobs, go to church, and serve the Lord. You also pray for married children to survive financially, establish a godly home, be able to conceive or to carry a baby full-term, be devoted, godly moms and dads. Or if there is a divorce in one of your children's lives, then your prayers are lifted again and again, "Lord, I need you to heal hurts in our family. I need my child to have the strength to go on alone as a parent with no spouse...to be a godly single parent."

Well, I'm sure you realize that on and on...and longer and longer...the list of our supplications and petitions grows! And the answer to our hurting hearts and consuming needs is to answer God's call to prayer and...*pray!* Only off-loading our stressful concerns by presenting them to our all-wise, all-powerful, all-sovereign—and all-gracious!—God, by "praying always with all prayer and *supplication* in the Spirit," will keep us in the eye of the storm. Only then...and there...will we know "the peace of God, which surpasses all understanding" (Philippians 4:7).

Checklist for Prayer

✓   *Pray daily*—Your needs arrive daily...and so do challenges and difficulties. Don't make the mistake of thinking you can meet them head-on, take them in stride, and enjoy victory *without* your all-powerful, all-wise, ever-caring heavenly Father's help! Be wise and ask for help daily. It's His day, and you are His child. And it is "through God we will do valiantly" (Psalm 60:12).

You need strength for today, and God promises "He shall strengthen your heart" (Psalm 31:24). You need guidance for today, and God promises to "instruct you and teach you in the way you should go" and "guide you" with His eye (Psalm 32:8). You need wisdom for today, and it's yours...if you will "trust in the LORD with all your heart, and lean not on your own understanding" (Proverbs 3:5). You need patience for today, and patience is His specialty, one of His fruit of the Spirit (Galatians 5:22).

And the list goes on…as does God's provision for your needs! Pray daily and ask Him for it.

✓ *Tithe your time*—Give God a daily time tithe. A spiritual mentor encouraged me to set aside ten percent of my "awake" hours to the Lord. Doing the math reveals that such a time tithe adds up to about one-and-a-half hours per day spent in these three activities that help a woman fortify herself for each new day and its challenges:

> Preparing—your heart for what's ahead by reading and studying God's Word,
>
> Praying—about the specific needs in your life and day, and
>
> Planning—how to best live out your God-given day.

These three daily exercises ensure that something is *going in* (your heart), something is *going up* (your prayers), and something is *going on* (your plan). It's a surefire formula for daily mastery. So whether you've got half-an-hour or an hour-and-a-half, give it to God!

✓ *Memorize Scripture*—More specifically, memorize Philippians 4:6. Write it on a 3" x 5" card, and carry it with you everywhere. Meditate on its rich instruction to your heart. As you follow its step-by-step directions, you will "find grace to help in time of *need*" (Hebrews 4:16).

Answering God's Call to You

Both Jim and I desire to be among those who pray. But recently we talked about several "things" we dearly, seriously, and for devout reasons desired to see happen in our lives and in the lives of our loved ones. I guess I could say we had been subtly slipping into the "shorthand" mode of "God-bless" praying.

So as a couple we purposed to contend in prayer about three specific and personal prayer requests. We decided to ask and seek and knock on the doors of heaven. We determined to entreat the Lord. We resolved to petition God for these items and to intercede on behalf of the people involved.

As you can well imagine, our prayers began going up more frequently and fervently, taking on a more polished and refined presentation. And then one day, after spending the entire morning realizing God's thrilling answer to one of our prayer requests, we walked out of the door...to a waiting cell-phone message that sent us instantly to our knees in tears of grief and brokenheartedness as we received an answer from God on another of our three prayer concerns. (And to update you, we have now gone Round Two on this same request...and suffered the same loss and heartbreak.)

But, beloved, what else *can* we do with an only-God-can-meet-it need? Answer: *Pray!* Prayer is God's avenue for us—for Jim and me, for you, for all of His people. So when *you* have a specific need...pray! God calls you to pray when you have a need, when something—anything!—is important to you.

Finding
God's Will
Through
Prayer

*When we practice the principle of making
no decision without prayer,
we experience a divine assurance
with every step we take.*

—ELIZABETH GEORGE

12

When You Must Make a Decision... Pray for Faith!

I'm sure you've had your bouts with wake-up calls. Well, believe me, one morning I received a wake-up call that helped me to further fine-tune my prayer-life. It led me straight into discovering yet another glistening feature of the gem of prayer. And what a life-changer and life-saver it is! Here's how it happened....

My day began in the usual way with early morning Bible reading and prayer, feeding the family, and getting them off to work and school. Then I started in on my day...and the phone rang.

The caller was the women's event coordinator for her church, calling to invite me to come speak at her church. She began painting a descriptive picture of the event—the ladies who would be there, the schedule, and the focus of the day, along with what she desired from me as the speaker. As she shared information, I noticed my fingers were impatiently drumming the table and my mind was anxiously wondering, When is she going to pause long enough for me to blurt out, "Sure! I'll come! When do you want me to come? I can come right now!"

When this gracious lady was done, I breathlessly assured her I would be delighted to come to her event and went on with my day.

At about eight o'clock that evening, our phone rang again. It was another sweet woman who explained that she was so excited that she couldn't wait until the next morning to call and ask me to consider coming to speak to the women in her church. As she spent time describing the event, I noticed that I was shaking my head from side to side and my mind was already rehearsing an answer of "No way! No how! No ma'am!" While I didn't say these actual words, they were certainly the words of my heart.

The next day during my prayer time, I sat before the Lord and wondered about the two phone calls. Each came from a godly woman. Each had to do with spiritual ministry. And each was for the same type of event. What had happened? Why my split responses?

As I thought and prayed about my distress over these two opportunities, I was convicted to the core of my heart when I realized that I wasn't making *spiritual* decisions! I was making *physical* decisions. Suddenly it all made sense. Prior to the morning phone request, I had taken my thyroid pill, downed several cups of coffee, eaten a scrambled egg and toast for breakfast, and finished a three-mile walk. Needless to say, my heart was pumping and my metabolism was in high gear! There was energy to spare!

And the evening phone call? Oh dear! I was already in my pajamas...already in my wonderful bed...with my electric blanket already on...ready to turn the light off after another long, strenuous day. I could hardly hold my head up to finish the conversation.

What an eye-opener! As I looked at the obvious reasons for the decisions I had made on the spot, I learned a valuable lesson—or two! As I said, it was my wake-up call to learn another key lesson in praying, which is....

No Decision Made Without Prayer!

Once God pinpointed my problem and why I had responded so differently in the cases of the two speaking opportunities, His Word came flooding to my heart. Example after example of men and women of God rushed to instruct me in the right way to make decisions.

—King Solomon prayed for wisdom to judge God's people, to "discern between good and evil"...and rose up from prayer to become the wisest man who ever lived (1 Kings 3:6-12).

—Nehemiah spent time "praying before the God of heaven" after hearing distressing news concerning God's people...and rose up knowing what action he had to take (Nehemiah 1:4-11).

—Queen Esther fasted three days and nights to prepare to follow God's will in a life-threatening situation (Esther 4:16)...and rose up to go boldly before the king with her request.

—The apostle Paul had prayed, "Lord, what do You want me to do?" (Acts 9:6)...and rose up to go to the city and be shown his next step into God's will by Ananias.

—King David was a man who prayed...and became a man after God's own heart who fulfilled all God's will (Acts 13:22).

—The Lord Jesus sought His Father's direction through prayer and rose up...declaring, "Let us go into the next towns, that I may preach there also, because for this purpose I have come forth" (Mark 1:35-39).

I have to tell you that, right there and then, I made a new prayer commitment: "From now on—*No decision made without prayer.*" To seal my commitment, I turned to a blank page in my prayer notebook and wrote across the top, "Decisions to Make." Beloved, this prayer principle of *No decision made without prayer* has guided my life from that day. And it can guide yours, too.

In the next few pages I want to briefly share how passing your decision-making process through the fire of prayer will help you live out a few of God's other calls upon your life— His call to faith, wisdom, and order. Then we'll look at a plan for making decisions that reflects the will of God for your life.

You Are Called to a Life of Faith

What's a woman to do about all of the opportunities, invitations, and decisions that come her way? And how can she know which things are God's will for her and which are not? Here's a principle from God's Word that will help guide us into a life marked by strong, powerful, confident faith. It's a guideline for making decisions and handling the doubtful things or "gray areas" of daily life:

> He who doubts is condemned if he eats, because
> he does not eat from faith; for *whatever is not from*
> *faith is sin* (Romans 14:23).

These words have to do with violating the conscience, with knowing when to move ahead in full faith and when to hold back because faith, confidence, and a clear conscience are missing.

In the flow of Romans 14, this verse is referring to Jews who were newly converted to Christianity. Their faith had not yet grown to the place where they could enjoy their release from Old Testament dietary restrictions and their newfound freedom in Christ to eat whatever they liked. The apostle Paul is advising that if these Christians doubted in their hearts or were not sure if an action was right or wrong, then they should not eat what was set in front of them. Doing so would bring about guilt and violate their consciences, which would be "sin" for them.

Exactly how does this principle of doubtful things and gray areas from Romans 14 apply to your decision making today? How does it direct you in your desire to live a life of faith and confidence?

1. *You are called to act in confidence*—You (and I and all Christians) should be fully persuaded and confident in your actions and conduct, believing wholeheartedly that you are doing the right thing in your endeavors. Such confidence adds unbelievable power to your life. Instead of waffling and wavering and walking uncertainly, you can act decisively and without qualms. However, if you do something that you are not sure is right or wrong, doubt sets in and takes over, weakening your confidence and bringing on the condemnation of guilt. Of course, you should always try to

obey what the Bible says. But when it does not speak specifically to an issue or is silent, then you are to follow your conscience.

2. *You are called to pray for confidence*—To act in confidence you must therefore pray in confidence *for* confidence.
Your goal is to live and act with the assurance that your
course of action is a right one. With this goal and purpose
in mind, I personally try not to make a move or commit
myself to anything until after prayer—whether for a day or
for months—when I sense clear direction, indicated by a
clear conscience and the absence of doubt.

3. *You are called to enjoy peace of mind*—When you pray
(and wait patiently on the Lord for His answer and direction!), you will eventually sense His clear direction. There
will be a clean and clear conscience. Doubts will be
removed, and your confidence in God's guidance will
blossom in your heart. When this happens after I've prayed
(for however long it takes), I can commit and say *yes*…or
refuse and say *no*. I can take on or decline a new responsi-
bility and move forward in the confidence of God. But when
the faith—the clear conscience, the peace of mind, the direction—isn't there, this teaching regarding doubtful things
comes to my rescue: *When in doubt, don't!* Or, put another
way, *When in doubt, it's out!*

Checklist for Prayer

✓ *Commit to pray*—Make your own *No decision made
without prayer* commitment. Write it out, remember
it, and rule your life by it. The surest way to miss
God's will and God's best is to not pray—to not even

pause, pray, and ask Him. And the surest way to be sure you discover God's will is, of course, to pray.

✓ *Set up to pray*—Make your own "Decisions to Make" prayer page. Purpose that from now on, every opportunity—to volunteer at work or school, to accept a wedding, shower, party, or lunch invitation, to sign up for a seminar, elective class, Bible study, or retreat, to use your home...or your spiritual gift...or your money...or your precious time and energy—*every* decision that must be made about *every*thing in your life will make its way onto your prayer page. Nothing is too small or too big to be prayed over. You are praying to know God's will for every detail of your life...and *that's* a big thing!

✓ *Ask as you pray*—Ask and answer these important questions when you are praying about doubtful things or gray areas:

> *Excess*—Will this practice slow me down? (Hebrews 12:1)
>
> *Expediency*—Is it useful, profitable, and beneficial? (1 Corinthians 6:12)
>
> *Emulation*—Is it what Jesus would do in the same situation? (1 John 2:6)
>
> *Evangelism*—Will it spread the gospel to unbelievers, enhance my testimony, or serve as a strong basis for personal evangelism? (Colossians 4:5)
>
> *Edification*—Will it build me up in Christ? (1 Corinthians 10:23)
>
> *Exaltation*—Will God be glorified? (1 Corinthians 10:31)

Example—Will this action offer my Christian brothers and sisters the proper kind of example—a righteous path—to follow? Will it harm my weaker brothers and sisters in Christ or strengthen them? (1 Corinthians 8:13)[1]

Answering God's Call to You

Thank you for staying with me on this important practice of praying for direction regarding the details of your life and any doubtful things that challenge your efforts to be a woman who walks with God in obedience, freedom, confidence, and power. It can be difficult to understand, but if you put it to work as you pray, it will be a lifesaver. I know it has been for me.

When I first became a Christian, I was enrolled in a master's degree program in marriage and family counseling. Everything went great...until I became a Christian and began reading the Bible. That's when my problem with doubt began. You see, much of what I was reading in my Bible was the opposite of what I was reading in my textbooks and being taught in my educational program. So doubt set in. And the effect was devastating. I loved reading my Bible, but I had to also read my textbooks. Finally I came to the point where I couldn't read either one. I was sick in my heart, confused in my mind, and torn in my soul.

A part of my distress was the large amount of money that Jim and I had put out to enroll in the current semester. And another part of my agony was my personal ethic of finishing what I started, of being faithful and diligent. So I had these two practical factors pulling on me to stay in the university program...while the truths of the Bible were pulling me to reject and run from the teaching of my daily curriculum.

Finally the day came when I couldn't read my Bible, I couldn't read my course assignments, I couldn't write my papers, and I couldn't go even one more time to subject myself to the lectures. I was most miserable! When my Jim found me with my head on my Bible, crying out to God through my tears, he asked what in the world was wrong. When I poured out my dilemma to him, he said, "Well, don't go back to that school!"

Of course I then asked, "But what about the money?"

And Jim said, "Let's just chalk the money up as the price of a good lesson learned. We will follow the Lord's leading in this, and His rule is, *When in doubt, don't! When in doubt, it's out!*"

Oh, how I praise God for the release that came to me through this precept concerning doubtful things in Romans 14:23! I cannot express the joy, the freedom, the relief, the peace, the energy that was mine from that second on! I never went back to the school or read one more word from my textbooks. But I was walking and leaping and praising God as I raced off to soak myself in His Word for as many hours of every day as I could! I couldn't get enough of the pure milk of the Word of God as I grew in the Lord. His Word was all I wanted.

Now, I want to quickly say, that this was *my* doubtful situation...at that time in *my* life and in my early growth as a Christian. If I were faced with the same situation today, my feelings and decisions might be completely different. And I also want to say that many of my friends, who were also Christians, took the course work, read the books, wrote the papers, completed their degrees, and are now licensed marriage and family counselors who are effectively and successfully helping other Christians to follow God.

Which brings us to the other part of God's message regarding doubtful things, which is this: When God shows us that something is wrong *for us*, we should obey and avoid it as a matter of conscience and personal conviction. But, at the same time, we are not to look down on other Christians who exercise their freedom and enjoy a clear conscience in those same gray areas. Romans 14:22 says we are to keep our beliefs between ourselves and God and be careful not to judge or condemn others by imposing our standard and our conviction on them.

Your sole goal, dear praying friend, is your own clear conscience before God. Why? Because you are called to a life of faith. That's a life of power and confidence. So when you have a decision to make...pray! It's not an option. It's a necessity! In the words of another person, "Prayer is the first thing, the second thing, and the third thing necessary for a believer. Pray, then, my dear Christian, pray, pray, and pray."[2]

*We are to consult with God regarding
every decision, word, thought, or response.
Before we move ahead or merely react,
we need to stop and pray first,
"God, what would You have me to
do, or think, or say, here?"*

—ELIZABETH GEORGE

13

When You Must Make a Decision... Pray for Wisdom!— Part 1

One of my passions continues to be the small-but-powerful book of Proverbs. That's because Proverbs is considered "the wisdom book" of the Bible. And I don't know about you, but I've already made enough mistakes to last a lifetime. Frankly, I would like to make as few as possible between now and my last days on this earth. So I can use all the wisdom I can get!

As I am writing this book, today is January 1. That means I began reading through my Bible again today. And because this is January 1, the proverb-for-the-day was Proverbs, Chapter 1. How refreshing it was to be reminded this morning from Proverbs 1 that you and I can...

>...attain wisdom and discipline,
>...understand words of insight,

> ...acquire a disciplined and prudent life,
> ...learn what is right and just and fair,
> ...gain prudence, and
> ...increase in knowledge and discretion.

How can this be? Because all of these elements of wisdom are available to us! We can grow in wisdom by reading, learning, and gleaning it from the Bible—from the book of Proverbs and from the whole of God's Word. We can also gain wisdom from wise people, teachers, and counselors, and from experience. There's no doubt that the wise woman takes advantage of all of these means for increasing in wisdom.

But here's a surefire, wide-open, readily accessible avenue for getting wisdom: We may—and must!—*ask God for wisdom* through prayer. It's as simple and as straightforward as that.

> If any of you lacks *wisdom*, let him *ask of God*,
> who gives to all liberally and without reproach,
> *and it will be given to him* (James 1:5).

You Are Called to a Life of Wisdom

In this book about making your desire to pray a reality and about answering God's call to prayer, we have come to decision-making and the will of God. And I have to tell you that what was meant to be one chapter has now grown! That's because finding God's will is such a crucial area in every Christian's life. To be a follower after God's own heart, we must *know God's will* and *do it* (Acts 13:22). Therefore, as we've learned, whenever anything comes our way, we first stop...and remember:

No decision made without prayer.

Prayer is *how* we humbly seek the mind and *will of God*. And prayer is also *how* we humbly—and wisely!—seek the *wisdom of God*. To discern and discover God's will in our decision-making, we must not fail to ask Him for it. That's absolutely the bottom line for acquiring wisdom.

The Workings of Wisdom

Exactly what does a life marked by wisdom look like? How does this powerful and crowning mark on a woman's life present itself in real life? And what is it that makes wisdom such an obvious indicator that a woman (*you*, I hope and pray!) is walking in God's will?

Wisdom fears the Lord—The primary insignia of wisdom is worn by the woman who realizes that "the fear of the LORD is the beginning of wisdom" (Proverbs 9:10). Wisdom fears the Lord!

At the core of a heart of wisdom is a desperate desire to know God's will…and to do it! There is a carefulness about life and a cautiousness, a fear, of rushing ahead of God's will…or missing it altogether. There is a deep respect for God. There is a "fear" of God, a worshiping submissiveness to Him. Therefore efforts to impress or please others or to serve self are set aside for one over-arching purpose and obsession in life—that of pleasing God, of finding favor with Him, of walking in His will.

And that's why we pray! We talk things over with the Lord *before* we act. We seek His direction *before* we make a move…or say a word. Why, we don't even know how to *think* about anything without God's Spirit and His Word prompting us and teaching us!

Wisdom applies God's Word to everyday life—Sometimes we don't think that a day is all that important. Yet in reality, all we have is a day—today! *Today* is all we have for doing God's will. Jesus pulled the reins in on all of our postponing, thinking, waiting, and wondering about tomorrow when He cautioned us, "Do not worry about tomorrow, for tomorrow will worry about its own things. Sufficient for *the day* is its own trouble" (Matthew 6:34). In other words, managing and handling today with all of its demands, quirks, and surprises in a godly and righteous and wise manner will require all of our effort, all of our strength, all of our focus, and all of our wisdom. We will be called upon to walk and act with wisdom and according to God's will all day long, around every corner, and in every encounter.

As the exquisite writer Charles Swindoll poetically puts it, "Wisdom is the God-given ability to...handle life with rare stability."[1] How was your yesterday? And how is your today going? Prayer serves as an edge and a border that keeps your day from unraveling. Therefore you'll need to pray yourself through your every day! You'll need to seek God's wisdom as the crises and curveballs of your day arrive as surely as the steady pounding of an ocean surf hits the shore.

Wisdom sees life from God's perspective—According to God's wisdom in the book of Proverbs, the fool envies the wealthy. The fool scorns his or her elders. The fool does not ask advice. The fool hates his neighbor. The fool sleeps his life away. The fool squanders his money. The fool despises wisdom. The fool speaks slander. The fool lies. The fool talks too much. The fool argues and quarrels...and there's more. Indeed, the list of a fool's perspective on life is long! But here's a fitting ending to it: The fool is arrogant and careless and does not want help or conceive of any need for it. In other words, a fool does not think or take the time—or even desire!—to view life from God's perspective and handle it with His wisdom.

Now the real question is, Are *you* seeing and living life from God's perspective? Beloved, *prayer* makes the difference! *Prayer* sets the wise woman apart from the "fools" just described. Taking time to close your eyes in prayer helps open them to God's way of seeing things. And be prepared—*He* sees life from a completely different angle. That's why wisdom is such a distinctive mark. It dramatically separates you from the masses. Such vision will make all the difference in the choices and decisions you make.

Wisdom follows the best course of action—It's easy to *know* the right thing to do. (The Bible says wisdom is calling out in the streets, on the corners, in all the public places—Proverbs 1:20-21. Wisdom is everywhere! It's available...and it's free!) But the final indicator of wisdom is to *do* the right thing.

That's why we must *pray* for a heart of wisdom. It's easy to be a fool...and almost impossible to walk in godly wisdom. That's why we need God's help. Unfortunately, Solomon, the wisest man in the world, possessed wisdom and *knew* the right things to do and could tell it to others. But he failed to continue to *do* what he knew...thus becoming a fool. Praying over our decisions gives our heart that extra boost when it comes to taking the best course of action.

Putting God's Wisdom to Work in Your Life

What can we do about prayer, wisdom, decision-making, and the will of God? I try to follow this scriptural for-mula...or better yet, *scriptural battle plan!*

First, I ask God for help. I pray, "Lord, Your Word says, 'If any of you lacks wisdom, let him ask of God...and it will be given to him' (James 1:5). So here I am, Lord! I need wisdom, and I'm asking You for it! Please reveal Your wisdom in this matter" (whatever it is).

Next, I pull James 4:17 out of my prayer arsenal and pray, "And Lord Your Word says 'to him who knows to do good'— to do the right thing—'and does not do it, to him it is sin.' Lord, I don't want to sin. I want to do the right thing. So I've got to know what the right thing to do is. Please show me what the right thing is so I can do it!"

And *finally,* I reach for yet another scripture for the battle—Proverbs 3:5 and 6—and pray, "And Lord, Your Word says to 'trust in the LORD with all your heart, and lean not on your own understanding; in all your ways acknowl-edge Him, and He shall direct your paths.' I don't want to rely on my own perception, so I'm asking You right now, Lord, to guide my footsteps. What is the right thing to do here? What is the right decision? What is the path You want me to walk in? What is the *right* way?"

Dear heart, these weapons work for every area of your life...and we'll see how in the next chapter. But I don't want these foundational prayer truths and practices to get buried right away in our rush to build upon them. No, I want us to stand back and admire them, to contemplate them, to appre-ciate them, to marvel over them. Better yet, I want us to embrace them and affirm that, "Yes, Lord, we will use these truths to help us find Your will!" If we went no further, if we ended this book right here, right now, you and I would have enough to build a life of devoted prayer. So let's make sure they are "built" into our hearts and lives.

Checklist for Prayer

To begin making headway on your checklist, first read again the paragraph on pages 144-45 that describes some of the attitudes and practices of a fool, of a person who does not see life from God's perspective. Were any of these true of you? As I've already shared, I firmly believe that a problem defined is a problem half solved. Therefore...

✓ *Pinpoint*...your Number One problem area—Name the one problem area you want or need to attack and eliminate right away. Put it on your prayer list. Then find out what God's Word and wisdom says about His wise way of handling this flaw. Look to the Bible first. Then seek wise counsel. And be sure to record in your prayer notebook or journal the scriptures that will help you fight your battle.

✓ *Purpose*...to pray daily—Your decision to tackle this problem requires the use of the arsenal of scriptures you are assembling.

Then graduate to putting away any and as many "un-wise" practices that are tripping you up in finding God's will. In these words, Proverbs explains the importance of "tending" the road that leads to God's will: "The way of the lazy man is like a hedge of thorns, but the way of the upright is a highway"

(Proverbs 15:19). Don't be so spiritually lazy that you fail to trim the hedge and remove the thorns that are crowding out your view of and access to the path of God's will! You must be able to *see* the way...so you can *find* God's will...and *walk* on the wide-open, clearly obvious highway of His will.

✓ *Pray*...faithfully—Any and all decisions you must make are important. You can begin by using the scriptures shared in this chapter—James 1:5 and 4:17, and Proverbs 3:5 and 6.

Answering God's Call to You

I hate breaking up this chapter. We were on such a roll and gaining momentum. We were successful in getting the groundwork laid. We were out on the runway with our engine revved up and racing, ready to go! But...if you're like me, facing a 20-plus page chapter can be the very speed bump that causes you to put a book down. And once it's down...well, an object at rest tends to remain at rest. Somehow it just doesn't get started up again because a 20-page commitment is required to pick it up again and go on. So I'm electing to break this topic into two chapters.

How I wish we were face-to-face, with our prayer notebooks in hand, shoulder to shoulder, sharing coffee or tea or a Coke...and most of all sharing our mutual passion for prayer! Then I could *show* you what it is that I do. I could *tell* you what has worked for me, just one woman who desires to pray in hopes that the fragrance of the Savior will sweeten my life and that of others. And you could show me your methods and tell me your secrets to being a praying woman!

I know that what I do won't necessarily end up being what you do. After all, you are God's own unique person with your own unique purpose and your own unique set of living conditions with its own unique personal and daily challenges. (That's why we pray, right? All the temptations to worry, feel overwhelmed, all the needs, the troubles, disappointments, pain...well, just read the Table of Contents!)

But oh, dear heart! my *grandest* prayer for you would be answered if what I am laboring to share, this attempt to touch upon the holy discipline of prayer, would help you be a woman who prays! I would be able to fall on my face before our Almighty God and thank Him profusely if my efforts helped you *in any way* to begin to pray, to improve your prayer life, to accelerate the prayer-discipline you already have in place, or to perfect you in making your desire to pray a reality.

May you act on your desires to realize this most important aspect of your life—that of being a woman who answers God's call to prayer...and who prays! If you do, you *will* find His will for your life...and for your every day.

*I have been driven many times to my knees
by the overwhelming conviction
that I had nowhere else to go.
My own wisdom, and that of all about me,
seemed insufficient for the day.*

—ABRAHAM LINCOLN

14

*W*hen *Y*ou *M*ust
*M*ake a *D*ecision...
*P*ray for *W*isdom!—
*P*art 2

*W*hat can you and I do to make better decisions regarding the issues and attitudes of our daily lives? And how can we come closer to discerning God's heart on the direction He would have us go in? How do we find God's will for us?

We began examining this all-important study of the role wisdom plays in decision-making in Chapter 13. Now in this chapter, I want to show you how to use God's Word as you pray to seek God's will. This chapter will be a very practical look at some of the matters that make up the days of your life. But before we dive in, let's review what we've already learned about "The Workings of Wisdom."

Remember What You Know

In the last chapter we defined four vital aspects of wisdom that are at the core of a woman after God's own heart—aspects that will help you walk in God's ways.

1. *Your relationship with God*—Embracing the Savior, selling-out to Him, knowing and loving the Lord, following and obeying Him, pursuing God and God alone, and seeking to fulfill His purpose for you. The cry of your heart should be, "Lord, what do *You* want me to do, say, or think? Thy will, not mine, be done."[1]

    —Wisdom fears the Lord.

2. *Your walk with God*—Being careful to think thoughts that honor Him, walk in ways that are worthy of your calling, seeking to please Him in your walk.[2]

    —Wisdom applies God's Word in daily life.

3. *Your desire to find God's will*—Nurturing a heart that is open to God's views about life and devoted to praying earnestly.[3]

    —Wisdom sees life from God's perspective.

4. *Your weapons for the battle*—Using scriptures as you pray to discern God's direction.[4]

    —Wisdom follows the best course of action.

Putting God's Wisdom to Work in Your Life

I promised that we would see how the use of these four aspects of wisdom will mark your life and lead you in your decision-making. They work in *every* area of your life. For instance, consider just a few.

Your relationships—Do you think you need to talk to someone about a difficult or distressing matter? If so, first remember *Step 1: No decision made without prayer.* Place your concern on your "Decisions to Make" page in your prayer notebook or journal.

Then remember *Step 2: Ask...and it will be given.* Begin praying for God's wisdom. Ask God if you really need to talk to the person...or if it would just feel good to get your irritation off your chest, to point out a shortcoming, to make your point, to get even, to let someone have it...or if you would learn greater humility by letting it go (Proverbs 12:16 and 19:11)...or if you are only thinking about yourself.

Stopping and waiting until you pray *(Step 1),* and taking the time needed to pray, search the Scriptures, and seek wise counsel *(Step 2)* can only benefit you. These two steps will keep you from rushing in and doing the wrong, unwise thing (Proverbs 19:2) or rushing in and gushing out the wrong, unwise words (Proverbs 15:28). They will also assist you in handling a difficult situation with God's wisdom, patience, love, and self-control, so that God's purposes are served and accomplished—His way! In short, they will mark *you* as a woman of wisdom.

I've personally discovered that praying about people problems usually results in tapping into God's great mercy...and then my heart is changed and I approach the matter in an entirely new way. Surprisingly, I begin to feel empathy and compassion for those I'm praying about. As God reminds me about the details of that person's living situation or physical condition, my insights are opened up. I become aware...or reminded...of their burdens and begin to give them the benefit of the doubt.

It's a sweet, sweet thing that happens to your heart when you pray before you act or speak up, when you look to God...before you leap *into* a situation and *onto* a person! It's a transformation. God's mercy does such a makeover on my heart that I end up praying for the very people whose actions drove me to pray in the first place!

In the end, the wise woman "opens her mouth with *wisdom*"...*if* she opens it at all! And *if* she decides to speak and address a matter, "on her tongue is *the law of kindness*" (Proverbs 31:26). Beloved, only prayer can accomplish these two miracles. Only prayer makes such wisdom and kindness ours. Only prayer can pummel our hard hearts and give us the lovingkindness and wisdom of God. So please, answer His call to prayer, and *pray* about your relationship.

Your finances—Is there something you think you should purchase? Again, begin by asking, "Lord, what is the right thing to do, the wise thing to do?" Find out what God wants you to do. Find out what His will is. Most of our purchases seem insignificant, but are they? So you again remember: *Step 1: No decision made without prayer* and *Step 2: Ask... and it will be given.*

There are many biblical guidelines about money (Number One of which is to realize that it isn't *your* money—it's *God's* money!). The Bible tells you how and for what you should or shouldn't spend and use your (correction: *God's!*) money. And these two steps—*Step 1* and *Step 2*—will buy you *time* for gaining God's insights into your prayer request.

And if the Bible doesn't speak specifically to your scenario, then you know what to do: *When in doubt, don't! When in doubt, it's out!* Or at least, *When in doubt, check it out!* Ask for advice. You'll also want to pray through the list of questions related to gray areas in Chapter 12. But if you want God's wisdom, He promises to give it to you. All you have to do is be sure you pray and ask Him for His wisdom with a heart ready to obey.

A personal story—Just this week I had to practice what I'm preaching. I have a very unique set of dishes that cried out for some kind of special silverware. Well, I *finally* found the perfect style...but it wasn't exactly cheap. Each box of four place settings cost about $30. Dear Jim gave me his approval...and even agreed they were just right. So...$30 x 2 plus shipping and handling...well, you get the picture. Needless to say, we never use these utensils without appreciating them.

Then one day I walked by a closeout aisle in, of all places, a military exchange, and there was *my* silverware...on sale for $9.99 per box of four place settings! I almost cried out loud, "Oh, no! How can this be! It's not fair!" And to make my experience worse, there were only two boxes left. It was only a split-second before my conniving heart began thinking, "Well, *every* homemaker knows you can *always* use extra silverware! You *never* have enough spoons! And they're so cheap! Just $20! Let's see, I went to the ATM this morning, and I have a $20 bill. And if it's a closeout, these may be discontinued, and there will never be any more..."

Stop right there! Now, what were those two steps?

Step 1: No decision made without prayer…
"Lord, in all my ways—and purchases!—I
wish to acknowledge You!"

Step 2: Ask…and it will be given…
"Lord, what do You think I should do about
purchasing this great bargain? What is the
right thing to do?"

It's not always this easy but, beloved, right there, in a
few brief seconds(!) I had my answer to my prayer to God.
I *knew* what the right thing to do was. From the recesses of
my mind and heart came verses I had memorized decades
before that day when I stood in that crowded aisle and
prayed for God's wisdom and guidance about a relatively
small purchase—"Godliness with contentment is great gain.
For we brought nothing into this world, and it is certain we
can carry nothing out. And having food and clothing, with
these we shall be content" (1 Timothy 6:6-8).

Now, dear reader, what do you think I did after receiving
an "answer" like this in response to my prayer for wisdom
from God's Word itself?

Well, I'm sure those knives and forks and spoons won't
be there the next time I go to that store. But…it's okay! My
heart is content for two reasons. First, I asked God to reveal
His will…and He did…and I followed it. There is no joy and
peace like obedience brings. And second, because I have
food and clothing. That's all I need, saith the Lord!

Hmmm, maybe you would benefit from memorizing
these verses from 1 Timothy 6:6-8, too, as you pray
regarding your (correction: *God's!*) finances and your purchases!

Your time—My daughter Courtney, the busy mom of three pre-schoolers, prays about each day during her morning prayer time. One particular day was her errand day. As she prayed about the hours and her chores, she asked God for wisdom, created a schedule, and then listed her errands and put them in an order of importance.

Later Courtney told me that at a point during her errand-running venture, she realized that not only had the three kids in the backseat lost interest, but they were about to fall apart. As she drove along, she prayed again about what the best thing to do was...and decided not to follow through on the final errand. In her own words, she said that one last errand would have been the straw that broke the camel's back and ruined what she hoped, planned, and prayed to be a fun outing for everyone.

But she, like you and me, *prayed*. And she prayed *about the details of her day*. And she prayed *about an order for the day*, even an order for the errands. And she prayed again *when things got hectic*. And because of prayer, her day—and her life for that day—and her activities took on the spiritual traits of strong faith, wisdom, and order.

Whether you are married or single, have a carload of kids, an empty nest, or no nest, my point is...*pray!* Pray about everything! Pray about your day, your priorities, your schedule. Then pray minute-by-minute while you follow your (correction: *God's!*) plan for the day. And pray when you have to make decisions and changes along the way. You are called to a life of prayer, to a life of faith, to a life of wisdom, and to a life of order. (Stay tuned for more on this lifestyle of order in our next chapter!)

Your job—Many women, both single and married, have difficult decisions to make concerning their jobs. They have to decide, first of all, whether to have a job or not. Next, will it be a part- or full-time job? Then, what kind of job, field, profession, work environment? And then there's whether to change jobs.

Oh, is prayer ever needed in such a weighty area! So in your decision-making process, you "ask the Lord in prayer." And you ask your husband, if you are married. Plus you ask mentors, both a spiritual and a professional advisor. And don't forget to ask your pastor.

And here are a few questions to ask as you walk along your path of prayer: Will this job (or a job) help me to move toward God's grand purpose for my life...or away from it? Is this job a promotion (advancing and moving me forward) or will I simply be maintaining the *status quo?* Will this job cause me to be away from home and family too much? Will it interfere with my spiritual growth, church attendance, or service to the body of Christ? Does it violate any clear teachings in the Bible? Does it pass the "faith test" covered in Chapter 12, or is there doubt in my heart and mind?

This sort of prayer process, this sort of discerning of the will of God, this sort of listening for the "still small voice" of God, will take some time. But take it! Take all the time you need to be clear, confident, and convinced of God's will.

Your parents—As your parents increase in age, so do your responsibilities. The day will come when you must pray about whether or not your parents should live near you or with you, or you should live near or with them...whether or not you should step out of your ministries, activities, and job to care for them, or look into hiring care or enlisting the help of a care facility...what to do with your parents' house and household belongings.

On and on the list of sobering decisions-to-be-made goes as you seek God's guidance about the best way to fulfill your daughterly (or daughterly-in-law!) duties. You will need God's evident direction and brilliant wisdom. So ask God for it...and it will be given to you! He promises that if you will acknowledge Him in all your ways, He *will* direct your paths.

Checklist for Prayer

✓ *Create a list*—Pinpoint the major areas of concern in your life. We have not even come close to covering every sphere of concern in this book. So make your own personal prayer list—include your thought life, your habits, your marriage relationship, your in-laws, your family.

✓ *Ask for help*—Seek God's wisdom with your problem areas. Create prayer pages for those hot spots. Allow your list to serve as a red flag signaling the parts of your life where you need God's wisdom. Then remember to pray about them daily, first thing...and on the spot when they raise their ugly heads!

✓ *Affirm your desire*—Commit to walk in wisdom, to seek *God's* will in all your ways and decisions. Keep your commitment fresh and strong. You may want to write out an updated resolution about the serious-ness and importance of desiring, knowing, finding, and doing God's will. Walking in His will and in all His ways will transform your life. You'll then bear the mark of His wisdom *and* the image of His Son. What more could a woman dream of...and pray for?!

Answering God's Call to You

As we leave this oh-so-brief overview of wisdom, please acknowledge the role wisdom plays in your decision-making process as you seek to find the will of God. I've referred to prayer many times throughout this book as being like a gem, an exquisite jewel with many finely chiseled, flashing facets. And wisdom is another one of those chiseled features in the glorious rock of prayer.

And, my dear praying friend, when you have answered God's call to prayer, when you have prayed, sought, and received God's wisdom and insight, and when you have made your decision, praise Him! Praise God that you can ask Him through prayer for His wisdom to guide your choices. Praise Him that you have done the praying and you have done the seeking, and you have made the best decision you can. Then proceed ahead with full confidence that you are in the will of God. When yours is a seeking heart, He can guide and direct your steps as you go. Then, all joy! Your life can bring Him the praise and honor and glory He so richly deserves.

Six Scriptural Reasons to Pause and Pray

Revelation of God's will—"Trust in the LORD with all your heart, and lean not on your own understanding; in all your ways acknowledge Him, and He shall direct your paths" (Proverbs 3:5-6).

Clarity of God's will—"The way of the lazy man is like a hedge of thorns, but the way of the upright is a highway" (KJV "is made plain") (Proverbs 15:19).

Discernment of God's will—"All the ways of a man are pure [and clean] in his own eyes, but the LORD weighs the spirits" (Proverbs 16:2).

Insight into God's will—"Every way of a man is right in his own eyes, but the LORD weighs the hearts" (Proverbs 21:2).

Blessing of God's will—"He who trusts in his own heart is a fool, but whoever walks wisely will be delivered" (Proverbs 28:26).

Patience for God's will—"Also it is not good for a soul to be without knowledge, and he sins who hastens with his feet" (Proverbs 19:2).

> *Lord,*
> *I realize that the choices I make each day*
> *are key to the way I live*
> *and the priorities I practice.*
> *Help me to make choices*
> *that will show it is You whom I serve!*
>
> —ELIZABETH GEORGE

15

When You Must Make a Decision... Pray for Order!

Have you ever met (or been!) a woman whose life is a mess? Every minute of her every day is chaos. She spends her waking hours dashing here, running there, forgetting this, losing that...all day long every day. There's never a moment's peace in her presence. Oh no! Everything's an issue. There's always a problem. Crises abound! She's always running late, arriving breathless at her appointments...full of apologies and weak excuses.

And the seriousness of this frazzled woman's condition goes far beyond explaining that she lives in a storm center— *she* is a storm center! Her *life* is a storm center (Proverbs 29:22)![1] Wherever *she* is, the *storm* is! And wherever she is, there is strife, tension, and a misuse of energy. Emotions boil alarmingly close to the surface. And, sure enough, they eventually—and predictably!—spill over and spoil her undertakings, the relationships around her, and any semblance of hope of a pleasant environment.

Well, all I can say is, *Been there! Done that!* Instead of being a mother, I was a "sheepherder," rushing my children out of the house, into the car, out of the car, into the store, and back again. "Hurry up! We're late! We're never going to make it!" ruled all outings. The agitation and panic surrounding each activity—from running errands to fixing a meal, to having company over, to getting to school, even church(!), on time—made for a steady diet of stomach acid, adrenaline, and nerves.

Oh, What a Difference Prayer Makes!

But then, as I began praying, two "miracles" occurred. Before I tell you what they were, think about the act of prayer. What are you doing when you are praying? Answer: Sitting...in the presence of God. Resting...in Him. Waiting...on the Lord. Worshiping...God. Meditating...on His character.

So, the first wonder (which became a breakthrough in my helter-skelter, slap-dash lifestyle) was that, for those minutes when I was praying, I was quiet, still, calm, at peace, and at rest. *Wow!* What a change of pace! What a difference prayer makes!

And the second marvelous thing that happened was this: *As* I stopped and assumed the physical posture of prayer, not only did my breakneck, adrenaline-induced pace slow, but my mind, heart, and soul wound down, too. And there, in the hurricane of all of the busyness of a woman's hectic life and my own futile hyperactivity, I found the calm at the center of the storm. I rested in the presence of the Lord. And while I was resting in Him and praying there near to the heart of God, I learned another value lesson for life—I learned that a woman is not only called to be a praying woman, but she is called to a life of order. And *as* she prays, the order emerges, casting its light on all her decision-making.

Order, then, becomes another mark of a woman who answers God's call to prayer.

Oh, What a Difference Order Makes!

As we've moved through the truths and teachings in this book about a woman's call to prayer, we have come to another section dealing with finding God's will through prayer. Prayerfully made choices, and decision-making through prayer, is aided by—and creates—an orderly life. An ordered life doesn't just happen, you know. You don't just wake up one morning and, like magic, your home, your family, your schedule, and your career are all neatly in place. No, there's no magic in an orderly life. It takes lots of prayer and lots of hard work.

So, my dear reader, what is needed to put your life in a condition where you at least have some idea of what, and who, to be praying for? Here are three critical elements that will aid you in bringing more order to your life. And as an added bonus, they will make it easier for you to find time to pray!

1. *Priorities*—When my husband teaches goal setting and time management, he often shares, "If you don't know where you are going, then any road will get you there." This saying definitely applies to the woman who hasn't prioritized her life. Every event, every outing, every invitation is open for acceptance. Everything has equal value. The only

limiting factor is making sure she doesn't double-book (which the person who lacks order does on a regular basis).

Does this sound like the frazzled lady from our opening? And how can this harried woman—and you and I—deal with our hectic lives? The answer is to prioritize. We must rank our activities and the people in our lives in God's order of importance. That's what priorities are all about. So the next question has got to be, What determines right priorities?

Right priorities begin with God. We can rank all the activities in our lives and have order or even an ordered life. But will it be in the order of priorities that honors and pleases God? *His* order of priorities is where our decision-making process must begin. That's why our top priority must be God. Jesus put it this way: "You shall love the LORD your God with all your heart, with all your soul, with all your mind, and with all your strength. 'This is the first commandment'" (Mark 12:30).

Do you want—or need—order and direction in your life? Then turn every area of your life over to God, purpose to seek Him and only Him, and ask Him daily in prayer to prioritize your day and your life.

Right priorities include serving others. Immediately after Jesus made the statement about God being your first priority, He continued, "And the second [commandment]...is this: 'You shall love your neighbor as yourself'" (verse 31).

Do you need to make a decision? Knowing God's order of priorities will help. It will guide you as you pray and plan each and every day: God is your first priority, then comes "others." But, oh, what joy and freedom you will have as you go about your day with *God's strength* and function in His will. You will be able to serve your family, your friends, your neighbors, your workmates, and the people at your church with *God's* abundant *grace* and *blessing*. Why? Because you put first things first. You prayed and sought to live your day according to God's will. When you and I put God first, we experience this truth:

> Put first things first and
> we get second things thrown in:
> Put second things first and
> we lose both first and second things.[2]

2. *Planning*—No dollar value can be put on your God-given resources of time, energy, and mental focus. Planning helps you make wise use of these resources. For instance, I *plan* to read my Bible every day. I *plan* to pray every day. I *plan* to walk every day. I *plan* what I will eat throughout the day. I *plan* on certain days not to start the car. I *plan* and list every phone call I must make. My husband and I *plan* family get-togethers and outings well in advance. Planning is a wise habit to develop and a definite mark of order!

- Planning rivets your focus on God's priorities. Prayerful planning reflects God first and others second...all day long.

- Planning makes better use of your resources. As a steward of God's resources, you must plan to use them wisely...all day long.

- Planning leads to freedom. Being spontaneous can be fun, but it usually costs dearly in time and money. Plan wisely in prayer and enjoy the freedom it brings...all day long.

❧ Planning keeps you from worrying. Time spent in planning is time well spent. If your day hasn't been thought about, prayed over, or planned for, you can't help but worry. Ask God to give you wisdom as you plan for your day. Place your plans into the capable hands of God. Why worry? Your plans are in God's hands...all day long!

❧ Planning leads to resolve. Planning and sticking with the plan gives you the godly "stubbornness" needed to resist temptation (like making that excessive purchase or proceeding with an unwise relationship)...all day long.

Dear friend, if you don't plan your day in prayer, your day will make its own plans. It will lack God's mark of order. It will look and feel like a day lived without prayer. And you probably aren't going to like the results. Those days without prayerful planning are usually the days you end up frustrated and defeated. To quote Jim again, *If you fail to plan...plan to fail!*

3. *Scheduling*—Planning tells you *what* you need to do about God's will and priorities. Scheduling tells you *when* you will live out God's will and priorities—when you will read your Bible, when you will pray, when you will do the laundry, when you will run those errands.

And just a word about scheduling: Certain priorities, like answering God's call to prayer and reading your Bible, must be scheduled (preferably early, and at the same time each day). Then you don't have to think about them. You just get up, get your cup of coffee, your Bible, your prayer notebook, and get started. You've scheduled God into your day as your Number One priority, and you've kept your commitment!

What a great way to start your golden day! You answered God's call to prayer. You made your desire to pray a reality. You lifted your decisions to be made up to God for His direction. And you have received some indicators of His will. And just think—it all began with a little thing like a schedule!

Checklist for Prayer

✓ *Pray over every activity*—There are plenty of activities that will vie for your time, attention, and energy. But which one or ones should you accept or attempt to accomplish? Put each one on trial. Pray over them. Ask God for His wisdom to choose your activities carefully and intelligently. What a glorious confidence in God's will you'll own in your heart when you walk into an event or activity *knowing* that it was chosen through and after much prayer!

✓ *Say no often*—In your life, as in art, less is more. You have prayed, planned, scheduled, and carefully laid out your day. Now it's time to follow through on God's will and your priority plan. And be prepared! This will require another round of prayer. You will need to pray now for God's help to say no...to your-self, to your flesh, to spontaneous invitations, to your excuses. Pray to God to help you make it through just this one day of walking in *His* plan—not yours!

✓ *Make graciousness a goal*—"A gracious woman retains honor" (Proverbs 11:16). How is graciousness to be accomplished? For starters, pray, plan, and prepare for a life of order. Read, study, and pray over the example of the ordered life of the Proverbs 31 woman. Look for role models of gracious women at your church. Pray to become a gracious woman who flows through her days at a pace that is unhurried, resulting in a life that is unruffled and accomplishes God's best. Such is the mark of God's order and will.

Answering God's Call to You

Beloved, the breathless, over-scheduled person is underproductive, constantly apologizing for being late, not doing what she promised to do, and feeling guilty. But that's not a description of you, is it? Oh no, not you, my praying sister! You are—or will be—a woman of order. Why? Because you have answered God's call to prayer. You are now (or hopefully soon will be) asking God for order to be added to your life.

God is never in a hurry, and neither will you be if you...

—Discover your priorities through prayer, the study of God's Word, and wise counsel.

—Develop goals that reflect those priorities.

—Draw up plans that will realize those goals.

—Determine your daily schedule through prayer. Then you will...

—Don your cloak of graciousness and walk in God's confidence, the master of your today... because it was born in prayer!

A Prayer for Living Out God's Plan

1. *Pray over your priorities*—"Lord, what is Your will for me at this time in my life?"

2. *Plan through your priorities*—"Lord, what must I do today to accomplish Your will?"

3. *Prepare a schedule based on your priorities*—"Lord, when should I do the things that live out these priorities today?"

4. *Proceed to implement your priorities*—"Lord, thank You for giving me Your direction for my day."

5. *Purpose to check your progress*—"Lord, I only have a limited time left in my day. What important tasks do I need to focus on for the remainder of the day?"

6. *Prepare for tomorrow*—"Lord, how can I better live out Your plan for my life tomorrow?"

7. *Praise God at the end of the day*—"Lord, thank You for a meaningful day, for 'a day well spent,'[3] for I have offered my life and this day to You as a 'living sacrifice.'"[4]

Out of the will of God
there is no such thing as success;
in the will of God
there cannot be any failure.[1]

16

When You Must Make a Decision...Pray for Understanding!

Yes, but...

Are these the two words you are thinking right about now? As you wonder about God's will and how to "find" it, are you feeling a bit uncertain about how everything adds up and fits together to indicate His will? Well, let's change your hesitation to three words—

Yes, but...how?

—and let me now share *how*. Let me give you the final step in the process I've been outlining for "Finding God's Will Through Prayer": You will know more about God's will for you and the issues in your life when you *pray for understanding*.

Discovering God's Will

It's hard to explain, but when we pray, we *do* receive direction and confidence from God. Somehow He is able to impress His will upon seeking hearts. Through Him we are able to understand what His will is. So I use four questions that I ask my heart during prayer. I ask these questions in my effort to seek God's answers and guidance. While I am praying about decisions that must be made, these queries lead me right along the path of finding God's will. Before I ask these four questions I run through a checklist.

Again, I'm struggling for words to share simply with you how I make decisions, but here's an attempt. It's sort of a checklist:

✓   *after* I run through the exercises regarding faith and doubt (see Chapter 12) and

✓   *after* I use my arsenal of scriptures to gain a heart of wisdom (see Chapters 13 and 14) and

✓   *after* I double-check my priorities against God's Word and my lifestyle for order (see Chapter 15),

✓   *then* I utilize these four questions as a final step in understanding God's will.

When I must nail down God's direction, and when I absolutely must discern and understand His will, out comes this wonderful, clarifying set of questions. These four questions help me to discover God's will for *me*, and I'm confident they will work for you, too, as you seek His will for *you*. After all, He wants us to know His will. Why else would He ask or expect us to do it (Ephesians 6:6)?

Four Questions for Your Heart

To begin your walk through these four questions to ask your heart, understand that honestly answering Questions 1 and 2 will surface your *motives*. Some of your motives will be pure and good, and others will be selfish and evil. After all, as Jeremiah pointed out, "The heart is deceitful above all things, and desperately wicked; who can know it?" (Jeremiah 17:9)!

Then, as you continue on with your decision-making through prayer, you'll discover that Questions 3 and 4 will surface your *convictions*—what you believe the Word of God says about your decisions. Here's how this exercise has worked for me.

Question 1: Why would I do this?—One day I received a phone call from someone in my home church asking me to lecture for six weeks in an ongoing series of classes. As I began praying and asked *Why would I do this?* I could hardly believe that the first response that popped out of my heart was one of those sinful, wicked motives. My heart replied in answer to this question, "Oh, my name will be in the bulletin! Everyone will see my name in the bulletin as a great Bible teacher!"

I don't have to tell you that such a response would never be a good reason to say *yes* to anything! No, the kinds of answers you and I are looking for as women after God's own heart include "because God would be glorified, because God's Word would be lifted up, because lives would be helped and changed, because I believe that the purpose of this lecture series is God-honoring." In these heart-responses we are certainly getting closer to pure motives and solid reasons for saying *yes* than I was with the sickening response that my name would appear in the church bulletin.

So what did I do with such an answer? I wrote it down on the prayer page I had created for this decision entitled

"Teach Women's Bible Study." On the spot, I confessed to my all-knowing Lord how *wrong* such a thought and motive was! Then I drew a line through the answer and placed the page in the "Decision to Make" section of my prayer notebook so I could look at it each day while I prayed about it...and record the progress being made toward making a decision—hopefully *God's* decision.

And why did I write down such an awful answer on my prayer page? Because if it came out of my heart once, it would probably come out of it more than once. And I wanted a record that God had convicted me that accepting such a lofty undertaking as teaching God's holy Word to His women for such a *sinful* reason would be *wrong*...therefore *not* God's will.

Question 2: Why would I not do this?—Here's another instance, one when I was invited to speak at a very large women's event. On Day 1 of praying about this ministry request (labeled "Speak at Women's Event"), I first asked *Why would I do this?* and recorded my answers.

Then I asked, *Why would I not do this?* And in rushed the answer, "Oh, I'm afraid! I've never done anything quite this large or in front of this many women! I'm afraid!"

Again, both you and I know fear is never a valid reason for refusing to do anything...if God is asking you to do it. Oh no! Our God has promised to supply *all* our needs (Philippians 4:19)—and that includes power in weakness and courage in the face of fear. Our God has promised that His grace will *always* be sufficient (2 Corinthians 12:9) when we need it to do His will. And our God has not—*not!*—given us the spirit of fear, but of power, and love, and a sound mind (2 Timothy 1:7).

Fear is certainly a factor that should be acknowledged and dealt with and prayed about. But fear should never be a reason for saying *no*. So I acknowledged it. I recorded my heart-response of fear...and then drew a line through it. I can tell you that *every* day that I prayed over that invitation, my heart immediately muttered, "I'm afraid!" And *every* day I was able to look at that initial answer with the line marked boldly through it and the scripture reference "2 Timothy 1:7!" written just as boldly next to it!

What if my answer had been, "Ah, that'll be a lot of work...or take a lot of time...or I don't feel like it"? Or "I'd have to give up golf...or shopping...or time with my girl-friends to do that ministry"?

Well, you get the picture! Write it down, whatever your lame answer is, confess your laziness and physical unwill-ingness to the Lord, make a mark through it, and go on. You've just surfaced a weakness (maybe even a character flaw), one that you'll probably have to deal with again and again as you seek to *do* (note the energy that is required!) God's will and to *work* it out—right down to the finishing point of your salvation (Philippians 2:12).

Now on to Questions 3 and 4, the ones that surface your *convictions*, what you believe to be right or wrong according to the Bible.

Question 3: Why should I do this?—When it was clear that my 93-year-old father had terminal cancer, Jim and I had a decision to make. We needed to know how much time I could—and should—give to help out and be present with him as he declined.

While this might be a hard decision for others, it wasn't for us...for a number of reasons. First of all, our daughters were both married and the nest at home was empty. Also, I didn't have a job outside the home, so my time was my own to manage, and it was available so that I could help.

But most of all, the decision was made easier for us because both Jim and I believed this was one way we could follow the Bible's command to "honor your father and your mother" (Exodus 20:12 and Ephesians 6:2). In other words, as a couple we had a mutual conviction about what the Bible said. Therefore, we believed I should do as much as I could to help.

My answers seemed to be lining up to something we could act on with confidence. We both believed helping my dad (who was 1,500 miles away) was the right thing to do. I had Jim's blessing, approval, and support. My daughters certainly didn't need me at home. We realistically faced the facts that there would be a sacrifice of time, money (for airline tickets and long-distance phone calls), and companionship with one another.

So off I went to Oklahoma. I was on the six o'clock morning flight from Los Angeles to Tulsa every Monday morning, and back every Thursday evening when one of my brothers took over for the weekend. Little did we know when we prayed, and when God guided us into His will, that those commutes would go on for almost one entire year!

But, dear one, *because of* the prayer process and praying to understand God's will in this major decision, we were committed to do what it took, to sacrifice what it required, to see it through, and to stand united through it. Both Jim and I had perfect peace of mind and heart. To this day we will still tell you that we have no regrets. And God's grace was sufficient for both of us during every minute of every day for that year. As the saying reminds us, "The will of God will never lead you where the grace of God cannot keep you."[2]

And I need to say this one more time: Your answers may turn out completely differently than mine did. You may be at a different season in your life or marriage. Your marriage partner may have strong opinions in one direction or another. You may have children still in the home. You may have a job that makes it impossible to do something like I did. So what can you do? *Pray!* Pray and pray and pray for understanding of what God's perfect will is *for you!* He *will* lead you to find it!

Question 4: Why should I not do this?—At one time I had an issue I prayed about long and hard. I agonized over trying to make some kind of decision. Finally I took the three pages of tear-stained, coffee-ringed, marked-on, rumpled notes out of my prayer notebook—the ones I had been using to record my prayer progress during the whole prayer-process on this particular item—and I took them to my Jim. As I handed them to him, I explained, "Jim, I just can't get any direction on this prayer request. Can you see if there is anything I'm missing?"

Well, dear Jim took not even one split-second to look at the request written across the page before he said, "Oh, you're not going to do that!" And when I voiced a startled, "Why?" he said, "Because I don't want you to do that."

End of prayers! Why? Because I have a very firm conviction that the Bible instructs me to follow my husband's leadership (Colossians 3:18). And I never want to be out doing anything my husband doesn't want me to do. No, I want and need Jim's blessing, support, and prayers. And more than that, I want to obey God's Word so that what I do pleases Him...with a capital H! I desire God's blessing and approval.

As I said, this is how this four-question exercise has worked for me. And now I'm praying it will help *you* to better understand the will of God for your life...and your every decision. You will want to use these four questions for each and every decision you pray about. I used my invitations to speak at women's events as an illustration from my life only because, as I shared earlier, that was what God used to show me an area of negligence in my prayer-life.

Ask these questions about *every* prayer concern. Should you sign up for a Bible study? Volunteer for a ministry? Enroll in a college or craft course? Continue to date a certain man? Attend the Saturday women's workshop at church? Join a gym? Spend Christmas at home or with your parents? Purchase a new bread machine? On and on the list of issues and concerns that make up a woman's wonderful—and challenging!—life goes. And for every single one of them, you will definitely come closer to discovering God's will by first determining *No decision made without prayer!* and then by asking these four questions for understanding.

Checklist for Prayer

✓ *Do it now!* Stop making decisions that you don't pray about! So far we've learned that a life of *faith,* a life of *wisdom,* a life of *order,* and a life of *understanding* are all realized when we pray. So do it now! Make the decision that decides *No decision made without prayer.* Begin putting every activity and possibility on trial through prayer.

Wow! Talk about becoming the woman after God's own heart that you've dreamed of becoming! Oh, dear one, prayer is the key! Prayer is the answer! Prayer is the way! When you answer God's call to pray, you become the woman He designed you to be—one who walks with Him in faith, wisdom, order, and understanding, one who walks confidently and graciously in His will.

✓ *Do it now!* If you haven't already done it, create a "Decisions to Make" section in your prayer notebook or journal...*now!* (And if you haven't yet created or purchased a notebook or journal, do it *now*, too.) It's true that "one-half the trouble in life can be traced to saying *yes* too quickly."[3] So instead of reaping "the trouble in life" quickly saying *yes* brings your way, pray!

✓ *Do it now!* If you haven't already begun, make a list of all the decisions you need to make. (I counted 14 on my list just this morning.) Then make a page for each one and place them in your "Decisions to Make" section. Then make your way through them.

And here's a quick fix along the way...just in case you are pressured for a quick answer: *Say no!* Realize that "when, against one's will, one is high-pressured into making a hurried decision, the best answer is always *no*, because *no* is more easily changed to *yes* than *yes* is to *no*."[4]

Answering God's Call to You

Please pardon all of my exclamation marks and the *Do it now's!* But, beloved, this is getting most urgent! For five chapters we have addressed the importance of finding God's will. We have admired the harvest of benefits walking in God's will reaps in the life of His women. It is now definitely time to do something. It is time to move out in action, to make your commitment, to build your notebook or purchase a journal, to begin sweetly saying, "I'll have to pray about that. Let me get back to you"…instead of blurting out, "Sure I'll do it," or "No how, no way, no ma'am!"

I stated earlier that God expects us to do His will. He even gives us the key to understanding and doing His will—"doing the will of God *from the heart*" (Ephesians 6:6)! Dear one, when making decisions, pray…and do a heart-check. The condition of your *heart* and your *heart's desire* is vital to understanding and doing God's will! So…how's your heart?

Discovering God's Formula for Effective Prayer

Here is the secret of a life of prayer.
Take time in the inner chamber
to bow down and worship;
and wait on Him until He unveils Himself,
and takes possession of you.[1]

—ANDREW MURRAY

The Time of Prayer

As a child growing up in a home where both parents were schoolteachers, an inordinate emphasis was put on learning. Not only were my three brothers and I to learn everything we could, but my parents continued expanding their knowledge, too. Even during the summer when school was out, one of my parents would go away for a week or two to complete graduate-level courses toward yet another advanced educational degree.

Well, not for me, I determined! I foolishly thought that when I graduated, *No more school for me! I'm out of here!* But now I know better. I now know what you know and what my parents knew: All of life is about learning.

And, as God so sovereignly arranged my life, I happen to live with a husband who has committed us as a couple to keep learning, no matter what. Jim keeps telling me, "Now, Liz, we're not going to get old." He says, "We're going to learn to use computers. We're going to master remote-retrieval telephone answering machines, fax machines, cell phones, voice mail, and digital cameras. We're going to learn to go online with email and the internet. We're going to learn whatever we need to learn!"

Every one of us is constantly about the business of learning how to do a variety of things, aren't we? We spend hours learning to use a computer, play the piano, paint, or quilt. I have one friend who goes one evening every week to take tole painting lessons. My daughter Katherine is learning to tint black-and-white photos with dabs of color. Another friend is learning the finer points of watercolor. Plus several women from my church and I attended a writers conference together to learn more about how to serve the Lord through writing. And one morning a woman called me from Alaska wanting to know if I had ever heard of a town called Sylmar, California. She had received a notice in the mail about a quilting conference in Sylmar and was going to fly all the way down from Alaska to sit in on this quilting class that lasted an entire week! She asked, "If Sylmar is near you, Elizabeth, could we get together for coffee?"

Learning About Prayer

Well, dear pray-er, one man has stated it well for us when it comes to learning to pray...and the time it takes to learn such a sacred discipline:

> It is sheer nonsense for us to imagine that we can learn the high art of getting guidance through communion with the Lord without being willing to set aside time for it and learn to pray.[2]

So far in this book we've looked at God's Word and learned some theology of prayer, the meaning of prayer, and the blessings of prayer. But our focus is switching with this new section. We are going to now learn about the practicalities of prayer, about "God's Formula for Effective Prayer," a formula we can—and must!—follow.

We are pressing toward the finish line, so hang on...and hang in there! There will be a new flavor to these fun chapters filled with motivating stories and practical helps to inspire your heart to pray. I like to think of this section as the "sparkle" the facets in the gem of prayer produce. The first component of God's formula is...

Choosing a Time for Personal Prayer

By observing God's people at prayer, we discover that a common denominator in their prayer-lives was a time, or times, of prayer.

- ♪ Abraham prayed early at daybreak.

- ♪ Jacob wrestled in prayer all night long until the breaking of day.

- ♪ Samuel, too, prayed all night long.

- ♪ The psalmist advised that we pray evening, morning, and at noon, day and night, at midnight, with the dawning of the morning, and in the night watches.

- ♪ Other saints prayed three times a day, even up to seven times a day!

- ♪ Jesus prayed in the morning, prayed through the night, prayed before eating, and prayed at midnight in the Garden of Gethsemane.

- ♪ Finally, we are to pray always (Ephesians 6:18) and without ceasing (1 Thessalonians 5:17).

It's obvious, isn't it, that to answer God's call to prayer, to make our desire to pray a reality, and to join this most worthy league of pray-ers, we must develop our own time for prayer. It can be any time, but it should definitely be a set time. For instance, there was a time when I chose early morning as my set time. At that season in my life, my children were pre-schoolers, which meant that if I didn't pray early, I didn't pray. Later when my girls were school-age, I switched my time to being the first thing I did after they left the house for school. So pick your time—the one that fits your lifestyle best—and then follow the three steps under "Checklist for Prayer."

Checklist for Prayer

✓   *First, get organized*—Set a time for prayer. Plan it, schedule it, protect it, and keep it as if it were an appointment. (Does this sound familiar?)

Can you remember dating a special guy and how wonderful that was? Can you recall how you relished the thought of every time you were going to be able to see him? You had a "date"...and a date on the calendar! Why, you were so excited that you put in extra time in preparation to get yourself ready to meet him, taking great care to look your best.

Well, the same should be true concerning you and a regular date with God to pray. This message came home loud and clear to me during one of my husband's annual two-week army camps. Jim usually went in the summer, but one year his unit went in the winter...right in the middle of February...to the state of Minnesota! That's because the Army Reserves were practicing the setup of portable hospital units in frigid snow and ice conditions.

At the camp where Jim stayed during those two weeks, a very basic-but-involved telephone system was installed for the troops. If anyone needed to talk to his or her spouse, an incoming call had to arrive at a specific time in the morning. That's because the one phone for the entire platoon was in a barracks that served as the command headquarters. So if I needed to talk to Jim, I had to call the one-and-only telephone number that served the one-and-only phone at precisely 5:45 A.M. That's when Jim would be walking by that one telephone on his way to the transport bus to leave for the hospital site.

Oh, how I prayed that I wouldn't need to call Jim! Yet, the occasion arose when I did have to contact him. So the night before, I set my alarm for 3:30 to allow for the two-hour time difference between the West Coast and Minnesota. It also gave me time to get up and get ready for the call, to splash cold water on my face, and drink a cup of coffee.

The night before I also wrote out a list of the questions I needed to ask Jim, knowing that *if* I actually got him, the transport bus left at 0600 (that's "army talk" for six o'clock) and there wouldn't be much time. Therefore, I got very organized so that *if* we had these few minutes to talk, I would remember everything I wanted and needed to cover. I even laid out a pen for writing down Jim's answers and advice.

The next day when the alarm went off, I tore out of bed, went through the waking-up drill, and sat... watching the clock, watching the clock, watching the clock. Finally, at last! at 3:44 (my time) I dialed in the special phone number. It rang exactly one time…and Jim picked up the phone and said, "Hello, Liz."

Now while I was sitting there with my heart racing in anticipation, sitting there waiting and going through all my preparations, I was also sitting there thinking, "Why can't I do this every morning to talk with God? Why can't I prepare to meet with the Lord in prayer the night before, get out a pad and pen, be organized about what I want to say to Him and need to ask of Him? Why can't I set the alarm, get right up and splash cold water on my face, have a cup of coffee or a glass of juice, sit and wait for that appointment with God, meet with Him right on schedule, and hear Him say (so to speak), 'Hello, Liz!'? Why can't I take the time and care to share my concerns with God in prayer and write down the answers He gives me?"

And the answer was crystal clear! I needed to *set* a *set time* for prayer…so that I could have a time *for* prayer…in order to have a time *of* prayer!

And, oh dear reader, now we are talking about *discipline*…and *a* discipline! So let's get disciplined! Pick a time and write your daily "date" with God right on your daily calendar.

✓ *Second, get ready*—Begin the night before and the morning of. It's true that…

> —the prepared person succeeds and the unprepared one fails,

> —75 percent of victory and achievement is traced back to preparation—maybe even 80 percent!

So, according to the wisdom of Cicero, "Before beginning, prepare carefully."

Prepare by *thinking about your prayer time…* about how much you look forward to it, about how important prayer is to your spiritual growth, about how crucial it is that your loved ones be prayed for, about the sheer joy of being obedient in this commanded spiritual discipline, about the unbelievable privilege you have to commune with and worship God in this most intimate way.

Then continue your preparations by *anticipating your needs* during your prayer time. My needs for contacting my husband included a quarter-hour head-start (for clearing my head!), some nourishment, a pad and pen—all of which I also need for my prayer time. Do your prayer needs include setting out your pen and a prayer notebook or journal and making a cup of tea? What else? I even read about one woman who feels like she needs to brush her teeth before she "talks" to God. Know what you need to do for optimizing your time of prayer.

Finally, prepare the night before by *getting to bed!* Schedule backward from your ideal prayer-time to allow yourself the sleep-time you need. Be ruthless as you bee-line to bed. And don't forget to set the alarm! Then pray…to get up to pray!

✓ *Third, get up*—And how is that accomplished? By getting up! I won't belabor the point, but I know people who sleep with their cell phones *and* telephones next to the bed. And believe me (and you know it, too), whenever either phone rings, they jump to answer! Their hearts are pounding, the adrenaline is flowing, and the blood is pumping...and they're up! (And it's just a telephone!)

This must become your response to your alarm's sound. Treat it like it's *God* calling you to prayer! It's your Commander-in-Chief. It's the Ruler of your life. It's the Master bidding you to join Him in prayer. So...get up!

Answering God's Call to You

My dear friend, although prayer is a sacred privilege, in some ways it is no different than any other activity you choose to undertake. Like my friends and my daughter and their interests in art—they wanted to learn about painting so they could enjoy painting—you must first want to learn about prayer so you can enjoy praying. Indeed, "he who has learned to pray has learned the greatest secret of a holy and a happy life"![3] Won't you answer God's call to prayer by the simple act of choosing a time for prayer? Then be faithful. Keep your commitment. Show up at the appointed time...and revel in the joy of communing with Him.

The Difference Prayer Makes

I got up early one morning
And rushed right into the day;
I had so much to accomplish
That I didn't take time to pray.

Problems just tumbled about me,
And heavier came each task;
"Why doesn't God help me?" I wondered.
He answered: "You didn't ask."

I wanted to see joy and beauty—
But the day toiled on, gray and bleak;
I wondered why God didn't show me,
He said, "But you didn't seek."

I tried to come into God's presence,
I used all my keys at the lock;
God gently and lovingly chided:
"My child, you didn't knock."

I woke up early this morning
And paused before entering the day;
I had so much to accomplish
That I had to take time to pray.[4]

*To flee unto God
is the only stay which can support us
in our afflictions,
the only armor which renders us invincible.*

—JOHN CALVIN

18

The Times of Prayer

A very sobering verse of Scripture that I probably think on daily is from the lips of Jesus. It was among His last words to His disciples before He turned His face toward the cross, crossed the Kidron brook, prayed in the Garden of Gethsemane...and encountered the traitor-disciple, Judas, and a large mob of soldiers and officials. He gave His loyal disciples both good news and bad news. He announced,

> *In the world you will have tribulation;*
> *but be of good cheer,*
> *I have overcome the world.*
> JOHN 16:33

Pain is a fact of life. We experience physical pain and emotional pain. But even in the midst of this "tribulation," we have Christ's *promise* that He has overcome the world. And as followers of Christ, we too are "overcomers" (1 John 5:4) as we draw upon His victorious strength through prayer. So, dear faithful praying friend, we must pray. We must decide to pray. We must commit to pray. We must discipline ourselves to pray. We must learn to pray. We must pray daily. We must pray regularly. We must pray diligently. And to do this requires that we have a *time of prayer* each day.

This chapter is about yet another part of God's formula for effective prayer—the *times* of prayer. There are occasions, sufferings, and perplexities—those *times*—that require extended prayer. I think by this point in our book, you have an idea of the times in our lives that have no solution and no means of enablement...except through prayer. Again, just recall the Table of Contents: When you are...in trouble, hurting, disappointed, worried, overwhelmed, or needful... *pray!*

Yes, we have periods in our lives when we need extended times of prayer—times of trouble, times of sickness, times of battle, times of distress, times when we have sinned against God, times when we petition God on behalf of a loved one, times when we are seeking God's will. That's when God says...

"Call to Me"

These words come from Jeremiah 33:3. The full instruction to God's prophet was, "Call to Me, and I will answer you, and show you great and mighty things, which you do not know." I've often heard this verse referred to as "God's phone number—JER333." And there are definitely those horrifying *times* when we will need to call God's number!

Times of emergency—It is during these crisis times that we must do what I once heard described as 9-1-1 praying. Do you realize all that goes on when a 9-1-1 call is made? The 9-1-1 emergency system is considered state-of-the-art.

All you (or even a child!) have to do is dial those three numbers and you are almost instantly connected with the emergency dispatcher. And in front of that dispatcher is a readout that lists the telephone number you are calling from and the name of the person it is listed to, complete with an address. Also listening in at the same time are the paramedics and the police and fire departments.

Callers to the 9-1-1 line may not even know what's going on. They're just calling in a panic. They may not know what the problem is or they may not be able to say what the problem is. They may not know where they are. They can be out of control and hysterical because something has happened to a loved one...or to them...or has been witnessed by them. But the truth is, the dispatcher doesn't actually need the callers to say anything. All people have to do is make the call...and help is on the way!

So it is with the times in our life when we are in desperation and in pain. All we have to do is reach out to God in a 9-1-1 call. Just like God said to Jeremiah, "Call to Me, and *I will answer you.*" Sure, sometimes we're hysterical. Sometimes we just don't know how to handle what is happening. Sometimes there aren't words to say what is happening, or there isn't the energy to say anything. But God hears. He knows our trouble. And help is already on the way! He has already begun to bring the answer, the remedy, the solution, the help, the grace needed when we call upon Him.

And this is what Hannah did when she had no child...and only God could help. Nehemiah called out to God when the city of Jerusalem, God's city, was lying in ruin and only God could change that. The church prayed a 9-1-1 prayer for Peter when he awaited death in prison. And Hezekiah cried out to the Lord when he encountered an

illness unto death.. Paul beseeched God—over and over—
regarding his thorn in the flesh, something that would not go
away, something that caused him great trouble. Moses raised
his prayers in the midst of battle. And our Savior poured out
His heart to His Father when preparing to meet death on a
cross.

In these types and times of trouble—and emergency!—
we must call out to the Lord in prayer.

Times of fighting for the family—There are also the
prayer-times when you must do what I call "going to battle."
These are the times when you roll up your prayer-sleeves
and take your privilege of petitioning God to a more fre-
quent and fervent level. The issues are spiritual, and the
people are your loved ones—your family, your flesh and
blood.

I personally keep a file of inspiring glimpses into the
prayers of others who loved and cared and prayed. Over
the years I've shared several of these in my other writings,
but they merit repeating for what they accomplish in our
hearts.

—One woman named Monica spent time in battle
storming the gates of heaven on behalf of her son, Augustine…who eventually became one of the great Fathers of
the early church. Augustine wrote in his confessions that "for
nine years, while I was rolling in the filth of sin, often
attempting to rise, and still sinking even deeper, did [my
mother], in vigorous hope, persist in incessant prayer. Day
and night the prayers of my mother came up before [God].
Her life employment was praying for [me], her son. My salvation was the constant burden of her supplication." For nine
years, dear Monica prayed for this wayward son's salvation.

Then shortly after Augustine was saved, his mother told him that her reason for living was over. She died five days later. Her battle was over!

—I battled in prayer for my husband, an army reservist, to not go to the Persian Gulf War. I battled for months for this prayer-cause because of the effect I believed it would have on the Lord's work (Jim was an associate pastor at that time), on our family life (both of our daughters were college-age...and dating men who might be their future mates), our financial life (his absence would mean I would have to get a job). So I went to battle.

I also fasted during this particular battle. When something is critical to you, something only God can settle or take care of or solve or intervene in, pray about the possibility of adding fasting to your prayers (2 Samuel 12:15-16; Esther 4:16; Acts 13:1-3). See how God guides you. The *when* and the *how* of fasting is different for each person and each problem. Just ask God. He will show you what is right for you.

—Evangelist Billy Graham's mother, soon after he gave his life to Christ at age 17 (for which she had been praying for 17 years), set aside a period every day for prayer devoted solely to Billy and the calling she believed was his. And she continued those prayers, never missing a day for seven years until the last uncertainty was resolved in Billy's heart, and he was well on his preaching way. She then continued to pray for him, though her prayers switched to a text drawn from 2 Timothy 2, that what he preached might meet God's approval.[1]

—Author Jeanne Hendricks was a speaker at our church's annual women's retreat. At our gathering she spoke about praying for one of her sons during late adolescence. At that time he went through what she called "a blackout period." Her cherished child was unenthusiastic, moody, depressed, communicating only in grunts and monosyllables. Mrs. Hendricks shared that this was one of the most traumatic times in her life. She said, "He was so far from the Lord, so far from us. I felt like the devil himself was out to get my child. I prayed as I never had before."[2]

And how long did she assault heaven with her prayers for that struggling son? For half a year! And for that same six months, Mrs. Hendricks shared from the podium, she had covenanted with God to give up her noon meal in fasting and prayer each day so that she could pray for one hour for her son until God broke through to him.

The battleground is the *hearts* of our children, spouses, relatives, parents. And the battle is *for* their hearts! When only God can break through and do something, we must pray! We must go to battle. So put on your armor and get into the battle for your family! Do battle through prayer and through fasting. The greatest thing one can do for another is pray for him or her. As I love to rephrase James 5:16, "The effective, fervent prayer of a righteous *woman* avails much."

Oh, for an army of women who see their life employment as praying for their family members—for their salvation, for their development into men and women of God who will put Him first! Christian women, take note! Devotional writer and lecturer, S.D. Gordon, commented, "If there is but one in a home in touch with God, that one becomes God's door into the whole family."[3] You, dear praying woman, are that *one,* that *door!*

Times of wrestling for the ministry—You are called to do battle for your ministry's sake. Wherever it is that God has put you to minister, dear friend, that place is a battlefield! You are in spiritual warfare.

And so are others! Edith Schaeffer wrote that it was at the first church her husband, Francis Schaeffer, pastored that she learned to pray without ceasing for him while he was in the pulpit. As the wife of the pastor, she felt praying for him *while* he preached was one of her most important responsibilities for both the preacher and the church.

Hudson Taylor, the great pioneer missionary and founder of China Inland Mission, taught other missionaries about the importance of learning "to move man through God by prayer alone," by praying for the ministry. He once wrote to his wife, Maria, and begged her to "wrestle mightily with God for me and for the work."[4]

Precious praying woman, when it comes to the work of the ministry, evangelist Corrie ten Boom pointed out for us that "the devil smiles when we make plans. He laughs when we get too busy. But he trembles when we pray, especially when we pray together."[5]

Times of distress and disaster—Just say these "d" words and you probably think of severity in our lives. Nelson Bell, the father of Ruth Graham, faced distress and disaster during his missionary days in China. For 20 years his family witnessed takeover after takeover, and upheaval after upheaval, as battles were fought and the leadership of the country changed. How did he handle his difficulties? He wrote, "I prayed constantly that God would help us bear the testimony and witness that we should. A faith and confidence exhibited only in times of peace does not amount to much."

Another "d" word is *disease,* which causes us to think of
cancer...which so often leads to "d"—*death.* When Edith
Schaeffer's husband, Francis, was dying of cancer, the substance of her prayers was, "Don't let any one of us stop
trusting you now, Lord. Please may our love be real for
you—solid oak, not a thin veneer. This is the time that
counts for your glory; don't let us blow it....Please, Father,
give us victory...."[6]

These examples instruct and encourage us, don't they?
When you and I pray in our times of distress, disaster, and
death, the substance of our prayers should include praying
for our faith, for our witness, for our testimony.

Aren't you glad that God's formula for effective prayer
includes lifting our heartbreaking, soul-wrenching battles
before Him, "the Commander of the army of the Lord"
(Joshua 5:14)? Praise Him that we have a place to direct our
prayers of anguish during those times when we must take
our cares *somewhere!* As our Lord said, even in those times
of tribulation, we can be of good cheer, for He has overcome
the world (John 16:33)!

Checklist for Prayer

✓   *Consider fasting*—I once read that Dr. and Mrs. James
    Dobson fast and pray for their children one day a
    week. I also personally know a couple who fasts and
    prays one day every week. This caused me to think—
    and pray—about what I might do in the Fasting
    Department...for every concern in my life! How
    about you?

✓ *Continue praying*—Don't stop praying. We are often tempted to give up praying for issues or for people. But we must remember that our timing is not God's. This was brought home to me again this past Sunday when our pastor's wife stood up during a sharing time and announced that her brother had come to the Lord after many decades of faithful prayer by her and others. Jesus reminds us that "men [and women] always ought to pray and not lose heart" (Luke 18:1).

✓ *Count your blessings*—It is so easy, especially in hard, trying times, to constantly be thinking about your problems, isn't it? The pain is all-consuming! But why not start your next prayer session by making it a praise session? Recount to God the many blessings He has bestowed upon you and your loved ones. Praise God, "for the LORD is good, for His mercy endures forever" (Jeremiah 33:11)!

Answering God's Call to You

"Call to Me," saith the Lord. This is a clarion call from the God of the universe to our hearts to call *unto* and *upon* Him! His call to prayer cannot be missed. "Call to Me, and I will answer you, and *show you great and mighty things*, which you do not know" (Jeremiah 33:3). In this call to prayer, you only have to do *one thing*—call upon God. Then He does *two things* for you—He promises to answer you *and* to show you great and mighty things!

So turn your heart upward! In your distress and your concern for others, call out to Him, the One who possesses all the power that exists...as well as all the comfort, mercy, and lovingkindness. Freely shoot your prayers heavenward. As many as you like! As many as you can! And as many as it takes! And then stand back, faithful pray-er. For the God of the universe *will* answer you. And, as if that weren't enough, He will also *show* you won-derful—incredible!—things that you do not know.

*Build yourself a cell
in your heart,
and retire there to pray.*

—CATHERINE OF SIENA

19
The Place of Prayer

I'm sure you've met people who impacted your life in important ways, making your time with them especially memorable. Well, that's what happened to me one wonderful weekend in the beautiful state of Washington.

After a women's event, I stayed overnight in the home of one of the organizers of the retreat so I could catch the first flight home the next morning. As Jennifer and I sat in her kitchen (where else!) and began to get better acquainted, she related to me the story of how she and her husband had acquired their home. They had purchased the home from her mother after her dad died and her mom decided to downsize and move to a smaller place.

Then Jennifer shared more details on a personal level. She said, "Liz, we remodeled the whole house. But there was one thing in the house that I couldn't touch, and that is this kitchen counter." She went on to explain, "All my life, every morning when I came down from sleep, the first thing I saw was my mother, sitting right here at the end of this counter, praying. I couldn't touch this counter. It was my mother's prayer place."

But the story goes on. The next morning when I came down the stairs that entered the kitchen, there was my hostess, sitting on a stool at the end of that kitchen counter with her Bible and notebook spread out, having her prayer time. You guessed it—Jennifer had made it her prayer place, too!

Is There a Proper Place to Pray?

As we have already noted, we can pray to God at any time, day or night. God never sleeps and is always available (Psalm 121:3). His ears are always open to the righteous, and He hears their prayers (1 Peter 3:12). But let's take our desires to answer God's call to prayer and to discover His formula for effective prayer one step further and ask, "Is there a correct or proper place to pray?"

Dear praying sister, true believers with clean hearts can approach God anywhere with their prayers. This was true in Old Testament times and New Testament times. For example,

> —King David prayed in a cave (Psalm 57).
>
> —The Israelites prayed in the wilderness (1 Kings 8:33-34,47-49).
>
> —Elijah prayed in an upper room in a house (1 Kings 17:20).
>
> —Daniel prayed in his room (Daniel 2:19).
>
> —Sailors prayed in their boat (Jonah 1:13-14).
>
> —Peter prayed on a housetop (Acts 10:9).
>
> —Lydia and a group of women prayed by the riverside (Acts 16:13).

—Paul and Silas prayed in stocks in a prison (Acts 16:25).

—Paul and the disciples at Tyre prayed on the beach (Acts 21:5).

God's people are to pray everywhere (1 Timothy 2:8). And that includes you and me! We can pray from *any* place, at *any* time. We can pray while we're working, while we're in the shower, while we're driving a car, while we're riding in an airplane, while we're down on our knees in a garden pulling weeds, or while we're at the kitchen counter…as my friend did.

My Journey to a Place of Prayer

I was just thinking through my own prayer-life, the journey I have taken into prayer, and the variety of my places of prayer. My first prayer place was the breakfast table, a nice big area for all my prayer "things." For years I did my praying there. Then some years later, I switched "my place of prayer" to the sofa. I covered the couch, the floor, the coffee table—every square inch!—with all my prayer paraphernalia and prayed to my heart's content.

After we moved, my next place was my bed. The electric blanket was there for cold mornings, and there was a good light. There was plenty of room in the nightstand for my Bible, prayer notebook, colored markers, and, of course, the Kleenex box. I could spread everything out on the bed—books, commentaries, prayer books, notepads—everything was right there. That was my favorite place to pray…then.

But as time progressed, I moved down to the couch in my little office. There I had a floor-to-ceiling bookcase where every kind of tool I would ever need during prayer

was available (until an earthquake demolished my office!).
My prayer notebook was there, as usual, front and center. I
discovered at this time in my spiritual life that when I was
in my place and in the process of prayer, I felt an urgency
to journal. So a little leather volume became yet another
"prayer companion." I wanted to chronicle God's promises
as I was reading them and use them when approaching Him
in supplication. As my prayer efforts evolved and grew, I
added a stack of 3" x 5" cards for writing down the special
requests I wanted to carry with me so I could be "praying
always" for those concerns nearest and dearest to my heart.

But I have to report that my notebook has been my
Number One mainstay and prayer tool for the 20 years I've
been on my personal prayer journey. I keep all sorts of
prayer "lists" in it. For instance...

I have a page for my own "personal list." Then I have a
"family list" and a "people list." We've already discussed the
necessity of a "decisions-to-be-made list." Then I have a
"maintenance list" for praying over the Christian disciplines
I'm seeking to nurture. I also keep a "spiritual growth list"
that's filled with resolutions and the lists of "alwayses" and
"nevers" that you and I both hope and pray will become
true in our lives! All the projects I'm working on are on my
"projects list," and ministry events are on my "ministry list."
I even have a "crisis list" for all the crises that are going on
in my life at any given time!

Dear praying sister, your prayer place will be different
than mine. And the tools you use to make your prayer-life
more powerful and efficient will differ from mine. But, oh,
what a thrill it will be to see your prayer place and your
prayer plan—and your prayer-life—evolve into something

that is organized and indicative of a serious pray-er, a woman who is making her desire to pray a reality!

The Places of Prayer for Others

Would you like to know how some others have prayed and where their places of prayer were? Let me mention just a few.

Susannah Wesley, the mother of the famous brothers, John and Charles Wesley, would simply pull her apron up over her head, and that provided a place of prayer for her. Maybe that's the only place she could find to pray (she bore 19 children, but 9 died before the age of 2)! Those ten children came to recognize their mother's apron as a "Do Not Disturb—Woman at Prayer" sign! (Do you have any children? And do you need to have an apron handy?)

John Wesley, the son of Susannah and the founder of Methodism, had a "prayer chamber" in his home. When Jim and I were in London as a part of a Bible tour to the Holy Land, we walked through John Wesley's home and actually stood for some time in his private prayer chamber, which has been carefully preserved exactly as it was. It was a little room off his bedroom. There was nothing in that room except a table with a candlestick and a Greek New Testament on it and a small stool—sort of a kneeling stool. The tour guide told us that this little room, this "prayer room," was "the powerhouse of Methodism." It was Mr. Wesley's prayer place. (Do you have a place or a room, or more importantly, a habit of praying, that others could point to as "the powerhouse" of your life, your family, your ministry?)

John Fletcher, eighteenth-century Methodist theologian, was said to have stained the walls of his chamber with the breath of his prayers lifted from his prayer place. (How do the walls of your prayer place measure up?)

The earliest male African converts to Christianity were quite earnest and regular in their personal devotions. Each man would go out through the bush to a private place to pray, and the routine of trekking through the grass marked out distinct paths as the grass became beaten down. One look and everyone could tell if someone was faithful in prayer because his path was obvious. But if anyone began to neglect his prayer time, it was also evident, and soon one of the brothers-in-Christ would come and say, "Brother, the grass grows on your path." (How's the "path" to your prayer place? Is it well used?)

Jill Briscoe, a writer, speaker, the wife of Pastor Stuart Briscoe, and a busy mother, used to put her baby *out* of the playpen, get *into* the playpen herself, and pray! That toddler's crib became her place of prayer! (Now, where can you get a play—correction: *pray!*—pen?)

Ruth Graham, wife of Billy Graham, calls "a big, old rolltop desk in the bedroom" her prayer place. Last year when Jim and I were at "The Cove," the retreat and conference center of the Billy Graham Evangelistic Association, a copy of the Association's *Decision* magazine was in our room with a note that basically said, "Take me!" And I took it! Why? Because inside it was an article entitled "A Special Place." That place, complete with a picture and a description, was none other than Ruth Graham's prayer place. Mrs. Graham's desk is littered with pictures of her family to look

at when she prays for them. There are several Bible translations, a Bible concordance, a handful of devotional books...
"and a mug filled with pens." Mrs. Graham believes in
leaving your Bible open someplace so that "whenever there
is a lull in the storms of life, we can grab a cup of coffee and
sit down for a time of pure refreshment and companionship."[1] (So...where can you squeeze in a cup of coffee and
enjoy some rich companionship with "the God of peace"?)

The Place of Prayer for You

Do any of these examples inspire you to find a special
place to pray? Jesus spoke of entering into "your room, and
when you have shut your door, pray" (Matthew 6:6). Some
would call such a room their "prayer closet," a place where
their prayer-life is nurtured. S.D. Gordon, in his classic book
Quiet Talks on Prayer, points out, "Oh! You can pray anywhere...but you are not likely to unless you are off in some
quiet place shut in with God." He advises, "Enter into thine
inner chamber, and shut thy door. That door is important. It
shuts out, and it shuts in....God is here in this shut-in spot.
One must get alone to find out that he is never alone."[2]

And here's another plus to establishing a prayer place.
Not only does having one help you focus, but it also fulfills
one of the rules of good time management: There are certain things you do in certain places, and when you get to
that place, you automatically know what to do when you get
there. In this case, the "thing" you want to do is pray, and
you want to be "conditioned" to do it in your place, thus cultivating a time of focused, concentrated, consecrated prayer.

Please, do whatever it takes for you to have *your* place
of prayer! Whether it's a literal closet or some other place,

discover or create *your* special place of retreat, the place where you go to meet with the Lord, where you go to pray.

$\mathscr{C}$hecklist for $\mathscr{P}$rayer

✓ *Describe*...your place of prayer—I shared about mine. Do you have one? If you are having trouble praying with all of the distractions of a busy home or job, maybe a prayer closet is what you need. (I have a friend who actually converted her coat closet into her prayer closet, complete with a desk and a book-case!)

 Or are you homeless when it comes to prayer? Or a vagabond...here a little, there a little, everywhere a little little? If so, then...

✓ *Decide*...where your place will be—Experiment. Move around. Sooner or later you'll feel comfortable and enjoy good success in your prayer efforts, and then your heart will tell you you're "home"! After our home was essentially destroyed in a California earth-quake, my fellow faculty wives at The Masters Semi-nary gave me a wooden book caddy...complete with a clip-on light...that I could pack all my books, pens, and notebooks in and carry around with me as we did repairs. I used that caddy for almost two years! Maybe a caddy would help you to begin your journey toward finding your place!

✓ *Provide*...what is missing—What would improve your prayer place? Think again about the resources Ruth Graham had at her fingertips. Talk to others and find out what makes their times "with the Eternal" most effective and meaningful. Then pray about what it is you need to provide to further your journey into prayer.

Answering God's Call to You

Many women spend hours each day decorating, cleaning, and maintaining the place they call "home." Many of these same women have no *prayer* place. These homemakers are homeless when it comes to prayer. But that doesn't have to be you. I'm asking *you* to take care of *your* spiritual life and "home,"—*your* prayer place. Get the juices flowing. Put your God-given organizational abilities and your "home"-making skills to work for you. Use them to create *your* place of prayer—the "powerhouse" for *your* life!

Man is never so tall
as when he kneels before God—
never so great
as when he humbles himself before God.
And the man who kneels to God
can stand up to anything.[1]

—Louis H. Evans

20

The Posture of Prayer

One night I was beginning a six-week lecture series on "A Woman After God's Own Heart," a class on prayer and praying about priorities. One of the women in the class had prayed well in advance that others would want to come with her to the course. Well, that opening night she walked in the door looking like a mother duck with little ducklings behind her! *Six* other women, both friends and neighbors, came with her to the class! There were so many of them that they occupied one entire table during that first session.

When I finished teaching that evening, I was busy talking to other ladies and packing up my notes and Bible. Out of the corner of my eye, I observed these seven women kneeling around their table…praying. They were making an instant, on-the-spot, application of the evening's content! They were committing themselves to pray for the duration of the course. That was one of their homework assignments, and they were *doing it now!* Their act of kneeling and praying was an expression of their commitment, of the giving of themselves and their hearts over to God. And their posture showed it.

How Then Should We Pray?

Many Christians, perhaps even those seven women, would argue that prayer should be offered on one's knees. These godly pray-ers would contend that kneeling is the biblical posture of prayer. They might even cite examples of Jesus kneeling in the garden in Gethsamene to pray (Luke 22:41). Or they might point to the apostle Paul kneeling on the beach with the elders from Ephesus, and with his disciples in Tyre before he journeyed to Rome (Acts 20:36; 21:5).

It's true that many throughout time have accomplished much praying on their knees. For instance, in the early days of our republic a stranger once asked at Congress how he would distinguish George Washington from the rest of the people. He was told that he could easily recognize him. When Congress goes to prayer, Washington is the gentleman who always kneels.

Also it was said of hymn-writer Fanny Crosby that she never attempted to write music or lyrics without first kneeling to pray about the undertaking. That meant she spent a great deal of time on her knees because she wrote more than 8,000 hymns of faith!

Then there is James, the leader of the church in Jerusalem. It has been passed down through history that he was known as "camel knees" by the early church. "When they came to coffin him, it was like coffining the knees of a camel rather than the knees of a man, so hard, so worn, so stiff were they from prayer, and so unlike any other dead man's knees they had ever coffined."[2] (How are *your* knees, dear pray-er?)

I have also saved a poem that further amplifies the use-fulness of praying on your knees.

$\mathscr{T}$raveling on $\mathscr{M}$y $\mathscr{K}$nees

Last night I took a journey
to a land across the sea.
I did not go by boat or plane,
I traveled on my knees.[3]

Praying on your knees is a graphic picture of one who is humble of heart. But, as biblical as kneeling may be, is there any other posture that you or I might use that would express our hearts to the Lord? Exactly how are we to pray physically? Looking at the Bible we discover a variety of postures for prayer.

— The people of God *bowed their heads* in worship as they heard that the Lord had looked on their afflictions as slaves in Egypt (Exodus 4:31).

— Moses and Aaron repeatedly *fell on their faces* at the door of the tabernacle of meetings, entreating the Lord in behalf of the disobedient and rebellious Israelites (Numbers 16:22 is one instance).

— Hannah *stood* at the doorway of the tabernacle of the Lord in Shiloh, praying with such passion for a son that Eli, the high priest, thought she was drunk (1 Samuel 1:12-14).

— David came to the tabernacle and *sat* before the Lord and prayed in utter amazement and awe that God had made an everlasting covenant with him and his family, with his "house" (2 Samuel 7:18).

— David, on the occasion of his young dying child, *fasted* and *lay on the ground* all night praying for that little one's recovery (2 Samuel 12:16).

— Solomon, the son of King David, *knelt* with his *hands spread out* toward heaven as he offered a prayer of dedication to God for the completion of the temple (1 Kings 8:54).

— Elijah *bowed down* and *put his face between his knees* and prayed for the drought to end and the rains to come (1 Kings 18:42; James 5:18).

— Jonah prayed to the Lord from the stomach of the fish (Jonah 2:1). (We can only imagine what his posture was during his impassioned prayer on that wild ocean voyage!)

— Ezra *bowed down* before the house of God, praying and confessing and *weeping* for the sins of the people (Ezra 10:1).

— The tax collector *hung his head* and *beat on his breast*, and in humility of heart *stood* afar off and said, "God, be merciful to me a sinner!" (Luke 18:13).

— Jesus poured out His prayers *on His face* in the garden praying, "O My Father, if it is possible, let this cup pass from Me; nevertheless, not as I will, but as You will" (Matthew 26:39).

The Bible does not give any definitive instruction on the "right" posture of our praying. But one thing is certain in all of the previous examples: These people were manifesting by their posture during prayer what was going on in their hearts. Some were worshiping as God's law prescribed. Some were torn in emotional agony. Some were suffering personally, and some were suffering for others. Some were remorseful over sin. Some were in battle, either literal war or for the lives and souls of others. Some were asking for a miracle. Some were joyful or thankful. Whatever the emotion the life situation evoked, it was expressed in the posture of the pray-er.

"When You Pray…"

Again, let me repeat: There is no right or wrong posture for prayer. When you pray, what is going on in your heart will usually dictate the personal posture of prayer that you choose to use. Emotion certainly has its place in prayer. It is a voice that must be heard and is stirred out of a sense of both a desire and a need to pray.

But Jesus has a word of caution for us: We must guard against using prayer and our posture of prayer as a means of getting attention. Both can also be distracting to others in a way that interferes with *their* prayer and worship. And prayer and how we express our prayers can so easily be done for all the wrong reasons. So be sure and check your motives for the manner in which you pray. Jesus advises us here:

> And when you pray, you shall not be like the hypocrites. For they love to pray standing in the synagogues and on the corners of the streets, that they may be *seen by men* (Matthew 6:5).

Jesus continues His instruction on prayer by giving a solution for making sure we don't use prayer as an avenue for "showing off." He gives this instruction:

> But you, when you pray, go into your room, and when you have shut your door, pray to your Father who is in the secret place; and your Father who sees in secret will reward you openly (verse 6).

Notice in both verses the issue is not "if" you pray, but "when you pray." Jesus assumes that you (and I!) are going to pray. His people are called to pray, commanded to pray, expected to pray, and instructed on how to pray. But the issue is always the heart—whether or not your heart is right before God. And, dear one, if your only desire is to worship God and praise Him and petition Him and pour out your heart to Him, then there will never be a wrong posture for your prayers. Why, you could even pray standing on your head, as the following discussion illustrates!

The Prayer of Cyrus Brown

"The proper way for man to pray,"
said Deacon Lemuel Keyes,
"the only proper attitude
is down upon his knees."

"Nay, I should say, the way to pray,"
said Reverend Dr. Wise,
"is standing straight with outstretched arms,
 with rapt and upturned eyes."

"Oh, no, no no!" said Elder Snow,
"Such posture is too proud.
A man should pray with eyes fast closed
and head contritely bowed."

"It seems to me his hands should be
austerely clasped in front,
with both thumbs pointing to the ground,"
said Reverend Dr. Blunt.

"Last year I fell in Hodgkins' well,
head first," said Cyril Brown,
"with both my heels a stickin' up,
my head a pointin' down.

"And I done prayed right then and there,
the best prayer I ever said,
the prayin'est prayer I ever prayed,
a standin' on my head!"[4]

ℰhecklist for 𝒫rayer

✓ *Be sure*—Are your motives for the posture of your
prayers pure? Are you seeking to call attention to
yourself? Or to the eloquence or length of your
prayers? Or is your posture of prayer the best way,
the most natural way, for you to communicate the
attitude with which you are coming into the presence
of God?

✓ *Be sure*—Are you spending the majority of your time
in prayer out of the public eye? Enjoy your times of
corporate prayer, praying for one another and
praising God, even praying in unison. These are vital
parts of "body life" in the church and of *koinonia*
(fellowship) among Christians. But be sure you spend
both quantity and quality time "praying in secret."
This will accomplish several things.

First, it will continue to affirm your motives for prayer. With no one to observe your posture or the piety of your prayers, you can commune earnestly and sincerely and fervently with your Lord with no prideful distractions. It's just you and your God behind that closed door. So pray, dear one, to your "audience of One"!

And second, a "secret" prayer life will allow you to focus on the real issues that need to be addressed in prayer. With no distractions, you can concentrate your full energy and efforts in a much more meaningful way. Your time in prayer can be extremely productive.

✓ *Be sure*—Are you a lady in all that you do? God's code of conduct for His women includes reverence (1 Timothy 3:11), graciousness and loveliness (Proverbs 11:16), and godly behavior (Titus 2:3). Surely His standards extend to your prayer posture!

Answering God's Call to You

Dear sister, God is calling you to a life of prayer. Prayer is one act of worship and service that you can give at any time and in any place. And like the women in my class, whose hearts were over-flowing with devotion and commitment, you can demonstrate your responses to God.

But as we have repeatedly agreed throughout this book, *prayer is a matter of the heart.* Your posture of prayer is an important aspect of your prayer-life. And that posture will change as your place of prayer changes and your reasons for praying change. Your heart and the specific situation will determine and dictate the posture that will envelop your prayers. Let your heart be your guide.

The fewer the words, the better the prayer.
The more words, the worse the prayer.
Few words and much meaning is Christian.
Many words and little meaning is pagan.

—MARTIN LUTHER

The Voice of Prayer

My husband, Jim, and I were recently on several book deadlines and had taken our writings to a sort of hideaway so we could bear down and finish our manuscripts. Friends had recommended a local church in the area, which we visited a number of times. So we were becoming quite familiar with the church and its wonderful people. But on one particular Sunday morning, we were privileged to be a part of an event that is now permanently etched in our minds and hearts.

The warm "aloha spirit" of this Hawaiian congregation with all of its customary greetings, hugging, kissing, and lively singing were a routine part of our visits to this friendly fellowship of believers. But on the Sunday that marked Jim and me, the pulpit was filled by a leader of the church while the pastor sat in one of the rows with the people. As the service closed, the guest speaker made a gesture for one of the older gentlemen in the church to come up. He was to offer a prayer for the pastor, who was checking into the hospital the next morning for emergency surgery. The man was elderly and almost had to be helped to the platform.

Well, as this senior saint had the ailing pastor sit in a chair in front of the pulpit, he invited anyone in the congregation who wanted to, to come up and surround their beloved shepherd.

And then he began to pray.

God's Voices of Prayer

What we experienced on that Sunday morning is a perfect example of what this chapter is about—the "voice" of prayer. That church statesman began praying back to his Lord much of Psalm 23. His voice was weak and raspy when he began. But as he proceeded down through the familiar psalm, using each verse of the "Shepherd Psalm" to pray for the pastor—the "shepherd" of the church flock—his voice grew in strength and power. He was not showing off or piously pouring forth pompous words. No, he was truly standing in the presence of his "great Shepherd"…and we had the privilege of listening in on his prayer to the Lord he had walked with for three-quarters of a century. This man's voice of prayer was so powerful and heartfelt that when he finished there wasn't a dry eye in the place…including ours!

Ever since that memorable day, as I read the prayers of many of the men and women in the Bible and "hear" and sense their voices, I can't help but think of the voice of this man's heart and the emotions it stirred in us.

I'm sure you've had your own experience of hearing the voice of an earnest heart in prayer. But we can also sense such heart-cries in several notable examples of pray-ers in the Bible. Imagine what emotion they must have exhibited as they poured forth their hearts before their God in prayer.

❧ Hannah—"wept in anguish" as she prayed in the house of the Lord. And as her soul sought to express the content of her heart, her lips moved but her voice was not heard...except in the halls of heaven (1 Samuel 1:10). But at the sight of her anguish the priest, Eli, took notice (verses 12-15).

❧ Ezra—voiced his prayer by "confessing, weeping, and bowing down before the house of God." His fervor and contrite spirit was so evident that the people joined with him in prayers of confession (Ezra 10:1).

❧ David—meditated on his bed, remembering the Lord (Psalm 63:6). Meditation's voice is one of thinking and reflecting, even praying out loud, all being done in private with only the Lord as your audience and the hearer of your prayer-voice. David carried on a conversation with his God. Wouldn't you like to have been listening in on *that* conversation?

❧ Peter—prayed three words, the Bible's shortest prayer, "Lord, save me!" (Matthew 14:30). Peter's voice of prayer was one of fear for his life. He proves that our prayers can be brief and to the point!

As I have repeatedly noted throughout this book on prayer, prayer needs to be a vital part of our lives. Whether our prayers are birthed out of anguish like Hannah's, or with reflection like David's, or even out of fear and desperation like Peter's, we need to be women with voices of prayer, women who lift up our voices in prayer. But you and I must not leave out the most important aspect of our prayer-life—our hearts.

Your Heart Is Your Voice

Beloved, it's true. You and I can say all the right words. We can use prayer books containing the eloquent prayers written by others. We can spend hours in prayer crying out to God. But no matter how important the prayer or the need, the key to the voice of prayer is the condition of our hearts. Consider these sobering truths—God will not answer when we...

> ...hold a grudge
> ...fail to forgive others
> ...fail to make our wrongs right
> ...refuse to apologize for our faults and sins
> ...are not kind and gentle to our enemies
> ...are jealous or critical
> ...indulge in known sin
> ...yield to temptation

How can I say this? Well, *I* can't. I personally wouldn't make a list like this because I would be looking for the easy way because of sin! But *God* can...and did! This is *His* list found throughout the Bible! (And there's more—this is only "the short list"!)

God has a few key words to share with us about our voice of prayer and its reception in the halls of His heaven. They're found in Psalm 66:18: "If I regard iniquity in my heart, the Lord will not hear."

Are you wondering, Is there any help...and hope? And, What, dear Lord, is it that I need to do for my voice of prayer to be heard by You? Psalm 34:17 and 18 tells us the answer: "The righteous cry out, and the LORD hears, and delivers them out of all their troubles. The LORD is near to those who have a broken heart, and saves such as have a contrite spirit." Psalm 51:17 echoes this same idea. Here David wrote, "The sacrifices of God are a broken spirit, a broken and a contrite heart—these, O God, You will not despise."

So the issue is, has been, and always will be the heart. It's not the *time* of prayer, it's not the *place* of prayer, it's not the *posture* of prayer, and it's not the *voice* of prayer. All of these elements are helpful and contribute to the whole of prayer. But dear one, it is the *heart* that makes all the difference in our prayer-life!

It's obvious that our words are not as important as our heart, isn't it? God hears no more than what our heart speaks, for...

> Prayer without the heart,
> The Lord will never hear;
> Nor will He to those lips attend
> Whose prayers are not sincere.[1]

All of life is about learning. And the greatest lesson we must learn, beyond how to better love God with all our heart, soul, strength, and mind (Luke 10:27), is how to pray from the heart.

Checklist for Prayer

✓ *Pray regularly*—The first step in "voicing your heart" to God is to pray! David said, "My voice You *shall* hear in the morning, O LORD...I *will* direct it to You, and I *will* look up" (Psalm 5:3). You will never have a voice of prayer...if you don't pray.

Once you have begun praying regularly, your next assignment is to learn more about prayer. Again, all areas of life require learning. I remember when I decided to learn better ways to clean my house. I bought a book entitled *Speed Cleaning*, read it, and then went out and purchased all of the items and products the book said would be helpful. I picked up razor blades, a toothbrush, a squirt bottle, just the right sponges, and an industrial apron...the whole bit! I assembled those items, and then I started using them as I put the principles of cleaning into practice.

The same with nutrition. I met with a nutritionist about a health problem, obtained her advice, read up on the matter, located a health food store, purchased the supplements, and started putting what I was learning into practice.

You will need to do the same with prayer, too. You must learn whatever it takes for you to better go about the business of prayer. Once again, we spend hours learning to play instruments and mastering other languages. We purchase things, take lessons, put money out for weekly lessons...or visits to the gym. Why not spend the time and the money to purchase whatever it takes to become a woman who makes her desire to pray a reality?

So if you need to purchase a book that guides you in prayer, do so. If you need to purchase a book of inspirational thoughts or the prayers of other people, again, do so. If you need to purchase a beautiful wordless book to inspire you to start writing down prayer requests and answers, do so. Whatever it takes to help you learn to pray and moves you to pray regularly, please do it!

✓ *Pray penitently*—Examine your heart. Remember, your voice in prayer comes out of your heart. Be sure yours is a "clean heart" (Psalm 51:10). As you come to prayer, do as the psalmist did. Ask God, "Search me, O God, and know my heart...and see if there is any wicked way in me" (Psalm 139:23-24). God is holy, and those who come to Him must have clean hands and a pure heart (James 4:8).

✓ *Pray Scripture*—The gentleman's voice of prayer at our church gathering was the voice of God's Word. God loves to hear His own words and heart repeated back to Him.

I know that when I have a heart full of hurts and concerns, my greatest joy and deepest relief comes when I pray back to God the "voice" of His own words that I have hidden in my heart. Many of these are what I call my "hands-off verses." They help me to voice personal confidence in God's strength, steadfast love, and care...even in my difficulties! Voicing words of faith (God's words, that is) enables me to look beyond the immediate problem to the finished product that God has in mind for me. A few of these "hands-off verses" are...

— Psalm 37:6: "*He* shall bring forth your righteousness as the light, and your justice as the noonday." As another translation reads, "*He* will make your innocence as clear as the dawn."[2]

— Psalm 46:10: "Be still, and know that I am God," or, as one Bible version says, "Cease striving and know that I am God" (NASB), meaning to "cease from warlike activities and acknowledge God's supremacy."[3]

— Psalm 56:4: "...In *God* I have put my trust; I will not fear. What can flesh do to me?" Although others may hurt us, nothing can defeat us!

— Psalm 108:13: "Through *God* we will do valiantly, for it is *He* who shall tread down our enemies." As one scholar explains, "With God's help we can claim more than mere survival, we can claim victory!"[4]

— Psalm 138:8: "The LORD will perfect that which concerns me." God will fulfill His purpose for us.

Answering God's Call to You

My dear sister-in-prayer, I hope you'll join me so that we may answer God's call to prayer together. Together let us lift our voices to His throne of grace! I know from personal experience that prayer and praying is not easy. Our lives are filled with a multitude of activities that tend to crowd out our times for prayer. And then there is the battle against our flesh. We struggle with sin and spiritual laziness. And since prayer is a spiritual exercise, we find ourselves fleeing from the presence of the Lord because of our divided, impure, and empty hearts.

So come, let us prepare our hearts—and voices!—for prayer.

The person who is about to come to prayer
should withdraw for a little and prepare himself,
and so become more attentive and active
for the whole of his prayer.
He should cast away all...troubling thoughts and
remind himself, so far as he is able,
of the majesty whom he approaches....
This is how he should come to prayer,
stretching out his soul, as it were,
instead of his hands,
straining his mind toward God
instead of his eyes.[5]
—ORIGEN

Developing
the Habit of
Prayer

Prayer isn't easy! It's definitely a discipline.
Three decisions can help you place
yourself before God
so He can fill your heart
with concern for others:

- *determine a time,*
- *determine a place,*
- *determine a plan.*

—ELIZABETH GEORGE

22

Ten Ways to Improve Your Prayer-Life— Part 1

When we began our pilgrimage into prayer, you and I set our sights—and our hearts—on answering God's call to prayer. The deep desire of our hearts was to make prayer a reality in our lives. And to launch our journey together, we took a look in the mirror and considered "Ten Reasons Women Don't Pray."

And now we have come full circle. We have examined those reasons...and hopefully done something about them! We have also looked at many of the circumstances in life that move us to pray—some that are inspiring and others that are distressing. Some of these were life situations that have no solution...other than leaving our requests with God, putting them in His capable and powerful hands through prayer.

So now I want to end this far-from-exhaustive book on prayer with yet another list—"Ten Ways to Improve Your Prayer-Life"—in hopes that the suggestions offered will encourage you to a more consistent prayer-life. Let's discover how to better develop the habit of praying.

1. *Use a prayer list or notebook*—How many times have you been guilty of telling someone that you would pray for them? At the moment you heard of their plight, you were deeply moved by their request, and your heart genuinely yearned to be a part of bringing their need before the throne of God. And then what happened? I'm sure that, if you're like me, more times than you would like to admit, you forgot about your promise to pray before you rounded the corner of the church building! Why? Because you didn't write the request down.

So, dear one, you can improve your prayer-life immediately…by leaps and bounds!…by using a list or notebook. Learn to carry a small spiral pad with you or a 3" x 5" card. Then, whenever someone asks you to pray for them or shares that they are struggling with an issue, and you are burdened to pray for them, write it down. Your next move is to transfer the request or need to your prayer notebook… and, of course, to faithfully pray!

(And P.S., if it's at all possible, pray with hurting people on the spot. Your spiritual response of instant, on-the-spot prayer can give them an immediate sense of relief, a God-perspective on their problem, and also minister peace to their hurting and bewildered hearts. Your act of bearing their burdens in prompt prayer proves that one person on the planet genuinely cares about them and their situations. Plus, I guess we could say that, if afterward you forget to pray for them…well, you did pray for and with them!)

And how about your own life, your own problems and concerns? A prayer list or notebook, although physically only paper and cardboard, is a marvelous spiritual aid to your prayer-life. It's a tool that…

🎵 orders your prayers,

🎵 helps you remember who and what to pray for,

🎵 serves as a visual reminder of God's faithfulness and goodness as He answers your prayer requests, and

🎵 creates a historical accounting of God's workings in your life and in others.

2. *Schedule a prayer time each day*—When you or I don't schedule something, it seldom gets done. It's definitely the same way with prayer! You can think about praying. You can talk about praying. You can worry about praying. You can wish to be praying. You can even pray to be praying! But until you schedule in the act of prayer, it probably won't happen. So tonight, when you plan your tomorrow and make your to-do list, include a time for prayer in tomorrow's schedule.

Do you remember our discussion about the "time" of prayer that British pastor Alexander MacLaren spent each day? It was one hour every day, and he referred to it as his habit of spending time "alone with the Eternal."[1] Well, my friend, his "hour of power" was from nine to ten every morning. Obviously, it was scheduled. It was settled that he would pray then, at that time, every day.

Do you have an "hour of power"? Even a "half-hour of power"? Maybe even a "quarter-hour of power"? I began my personal journey into prayer with five minutes a day, a "one-twelfth hour of power"! My principle was *something is better than nothing!* So I aimed at something. I found at that time that if I aimed at the one hour, I could find 1,001 reasons why I couldn't stop what I was doing and spend that hour. After I found myself going to bed night after night and missing the prayer time I so desired and so needed, I decided something is better than nothing in the Prayer Department!

My five minutes became the bait that drew me into experiencing sweet, precious times of prayer, many of those times extending on and on! Forget the clock! Once I was started, I couldn't stop! Sure, there were those days when five minutes was all there was...or a crying baby made sure that was all there was. But I began small...and, in time, witnessed mighty effects! And, my reading friend, the same will be true for you when you schedule a prayer time each day.

Speaking of babies and little ones, I simply can't resist sharing this delightful story!

How one woman "learned" to pray—Dr. Henrietta Mears, the legendary Christian education director of Hollywood Presbyterian Church, told her students how she learned to pray. She said that every day her mother spent an hour on her knees in personal prayer. She closed herself up in her room and no one would dream of violating her privacy...no one except her little rambunctious daughter Henrietta!

And so Henrietta would run in and out. She would kneel down beside her mother, and her mother would put her arm around her little one's shoulders and offer up some kind of prayer for Henrietta—that the Lord would make her a good girl, that the Lord would watch over her, guide her. And then Henrietta would get up and run about her business.

As a child, Henrietta Mears' great ambition in life was to spend an hour in prayer, just like her mother did. So one morning she got the great big alarm clock and went in and put it down on her bedspread and knelt beside the bed to pray, closed her eyes, and started praying. And she prayed, and prayed and prayed! She prayed for everything she could think of! Then she paused and thought, prayed some more, and then peeked at the clock to see how she was doing...and one whole minute had passed! What, she wondered, did her mother think of to pray for a whole hour everyday?[2]

We, too, need a set time, and an extended time, for prayer. Like Henrietta Mears' mother, and later Miss Mears herself, we move forward in developing the habit of prayer when we schedule a prayer-time each day.

3. *Spend time praying with others*—The habit of praying is born and nurtured in private, "alone with the Eternal." However, group prayer and corporate prayer are two additional prayer-practices that can mature and enhance your prayer-life.

Group prayer. Do you know some sisters-in-Christ who share your heart for prayer? Perhaps you could establish a prayer group with those women. Or perhaps, with their help, you could set up an organized time of prayer for those women in your church who share your passion. Your group could meet at the church, or on a rotating basis in the homes of the group members, or even in a park! Just be sure the gathering is organized and structured so the group's time and the quantity and quality of their prayer needs and purposes are maximized. The only caution would be that the group prayer sessions don't degenerate into group gossip sessions. That's one boundary or rule you'll want to be sure to establish.

Corporate prayer. I've been involved on several occasions in "all night prayer vigils" that were organized by the woman's ministry at my church. On one of those occasions, my friend Judy (who is a pray-er *and* a prayer-warrior!) led the group through a steady stream of prayer prompts and subjects for prayer and scriptures to use during prayer. Microphones were set up in the aisles so women could quietly come forward and offer their heartfelt prayers on behalf of the prayer concerns and prayer "business" of the group. It was thrilling to put self aside and dedicate extended time to praying for the needs of the church, its leaders, our missionaries, our nation, and the world. What a joy to hear hundreds of women turning in their Bibles to look up the scriptures as they prepared to pray, and then to listen in and join in on their petitions to God as they answered His call to pray as a body of believers.

4. *Pray using Scripture*—God not only loves to hear His own Word, but there is power in His Word. Indeed, "the word of God is living and powerful, and sharper than any two-edged sword" (Hebrews 4:12)! So make it a goal to incorporate the Scriptures into your prayers.

For years, I, along with many of my praying friends at church, used a little book entitled *Drawing Near* to aid me in personal prayer. It was a tiny, leather-bound volume that consisted of scriptures to be used during prayer. It was God's Word arranged in prayer prompts for adoration and confession and praise and supplication. But the arranger of those prayer-scriptures produced an even better book. It is a three-month prayer guide by Kenneth Boa, called simply *A Handbook of Prayer*,[3] and it was my privilege to endorse this book. To use it, you simply turn to the day of the month and begin to pray through the scriptures and the prayer prompts there...and off you go on your own adventure into prayer!

And here's another help. Over the years I have developed the habit of "color coding" different verses in my Bible with highlighter pens. These multicolored verses become my prompts as I pray down through my Bible, spotting and praying certain colored verses for the different areas and disciplines that pertain to my life and prayer concerns.

And I can't resist one more help! Try inserting people's names into verses of Scripture. I have an old denim-covered prayer book called "Pocket Prayers" that is, once again, nothing but Scripture passages with blank lines in the text for inserting whoever's name comes to your mind when you are praying those particular scriptures, or for including the name of the person you are carrying in your heart and feel burdened to pray for. I especially used these Scripture-prayers for my daughters, inserting their names as they were growing up, along with praying them for Jim and me. And now I use them for my grandchildren!

5. *Borrow from the prayers of others*—You and I can—and should!—lift up spontaneous prayers on a continuous basis and covering a variety of issues. Certainly such offerings come from hearts filled with love and gratitude. But many times these prayers lack order and clarity. They are arrow-prayers shot heavenward. But our praying shouldn't stop there!

It's a good exercise at times to read and pray through the written prayers of others who have obviously spent countless hours crafting and writing prayers in the same areas of our heartfelt longings and desires. These powerful prayers from the saints of old can be used to bombard heaven like heavy artillery! They help us to grow in our prayer skills and passion, and improve our "prayer language" by their eloquence and mastery of the English language.

There are many collections of poignant, moving prayers in print, but one book that has been of great inspiration to me is *The Valley of Vision,* a collection of Puritan prayers and devotions. (I've included it and several other volumes in a bibliography in the back of this book.) "Listen" as you read, if you will, to just one portion of one of these incredible Puritan prayers from a section labeled "Longings After God." See if you, too, don't come away from this prayer with a "longing after God."

Blessed Lord, let me climb up near to thee,
and love, and long, and plead, and wrestle with thee,
and pant for deliverance from the body of sin,
for my heart is wandering and lifeless,
and my soul mourns to think
it should ever lose sight of its beloved.
Wrap my life in divine love, and
keep me ever desiring thee,
always humble and resigned to thy will,
more fixed on thyself,
that I may be more fitted for [serving].[4]

Checklist for Prayer

✓ *Pray with others*—I won't mention your prayer note-book again, or the discipline of scheduling your prayer time (...or should I?). But I do want to ask you to consider expanding your life of prayer by praying with others who are like-minded and like-hearted. When you are with others at church, listen as they talk. When you hear people share who sound like they have vital prayer lives, get together with them. Then maybe the two of you can begin a prayer group together!

✓ *Pray using Scripture*—List three of your favorite scriptures that could be used as prayer tools for your own spiritual growth and on behalf of others. You'll want to memorize them...and then put them to use in your daily prayer times. If you can't think of any, begin with Colossians 1:9-14.

✓ *Pray the prayers of others*—Check out the list of prayer books at the end of this book. Do any sound appealing to you? Call your Christian bookstore, or get on-line with a Christian book distributor, or talk to others about their favorite books of prayers. Then borrow one or order one...and pray away!

Answering God's Call to You

Dear one, you (and I) are called to pray... period. You are to pray alone, to shut your door and pray to your Father in secret (Matthew 6:6). You are to pray with a handful of faithful others, like Daniel probably did with his three friends (Daniel 1:17-18) and like Paul and Silas did (Acts 16:25). And you are to pray along with others as a corporate body like the 120 disciples of Christ did while gathered in an upper room (Acts 1:13-15). As we'll see in our final chapter, prayer is all-encompassing. It is to be such a vital part of your life that you are praying at all times, in all ways, for all people.

Whether you run a business...or a home...or a ministry, you have to be organized, alert, and growing. And, dear beloved praying friend, that's what these five ways to improve your prayer-life will accomplish as you run your prayer-life. So, like a businesswoman, get your notebook up and running. Be organized when it comes to scheduling prayer. Spend time with others and find out how they pray. Make use of the "manual," the Bible. And grow through the writings and experiences of others. Make your desire to pray a reality!

*We must begin and end every day
with praising God,
we must give Him thanks every morning
for the mercies of the night and
every night for the mercies of the day;
going out and coming in, we must bless God.*[1]

—MATTHEW HENRY

23

Ten Ways to Improve Your Prayer-Life— Part 2

Can you think back with me for a minute to Chapter 7? If you remember, that was our up-close-and-personal look at King David's prayers and prayer-life in the wake of being betrayed by his son and a close friend, along with being ousted from his home and kingdom. At that time David, the warrior and *prayer*-warrior(!), testified, "Evening and morning and at noon I will pray, and cry aloud" (Psalm 55:17).

What I love about David's prayer-life, and what made it most powerful, is the fact that David had developed the habit of prayer. He is the man who declared to God, "My voice You *shall* hear in the morning, O LORD; in the morning I *will* direct it to You, and I *will* look up" (Psalm 5:3).

Then when trouble arrived, David simply turned up the steam on his prayer-habit. All he had to do in order to do battle through prayer was kick up the heat a notch...or two! He didn't have to begin praying, or learn to pray, or determine that he needed to pray, or would pray, or should pray.

No, he simply increased the intensity, frequency, and the fervor of his prayers.

How could he do that? Because the discipline of prayer was already in place as a vital part of David's life. The habit of praying was already developed. So he went, we might say, from morning prayers...to morning, noon, *and* evening prayers. In other words, he went into battle mode! The biggest mistake David's enemies ever made was forcing God's servant to pray *more* because, as David confidently testified of God's involvement and response, "He shall hear my voice" (Psalm 55:17)!

In our last chapter we began our list of "Ten Ways to Improve Your Prayer Life." And now it's time to add more "ways" to pray so that the habit of prayer becomes deeply ingrained in *your* soul...and *your* days...and *your* life!

6. *Open and close each day with a time of prayer*—I know I mentioned Susannah Wesley and her apron earlier. But what a joy it was to my heart to read again about her prayer-life. Not only did this godly woman throw her apron over her head periodically throughout her busy days for moments of prayer, but she also maintained the habit of having her private devotions and prayer time first thing each morning, from five to six o'clock. She expressed the wish that she not be disturbed during that hour, and, oddly enough, her wish was granted![2]

But there's more! "When Susannah was about thirty years old, with her demanding brood around her, she had adopted the practice of observing an hour of solitary meditation *in the early morning*—and very early it was—and also *in the evening*. Later in life she added a noonday period. Nothing was allowed to interfere with this schedule, for she believed that such times of solitary communion were essential if she were to play her exacting role with the composure and self-control it required."[3]

Morning and evening. You may not be able to incorporate the amount of time our dear Mrs. Wesley did, but you can develop the habit of beginning and ending each day with prayer. First thing...and last thing! First word...and last word! They belong to God.

A favorite psalm of mine speaks of declaring "Your lovingkindness *in the morning*, and Your faithfulness *every night*" (Psalm 92:2). Such prayers have been labeled "dawn and dusk bookends." And, as a familiar "anonymous" teaching suggests, "In the morning, prayer is the key that opens to us the treasures of God's mercies and blessings; in the evening, it is the key that shuts us up under His protection and safeguard."[4] Put succinctly, "Prayer is the key of the morning and the bolt of the night."[5]

7. *Gain inspiration from the biographies of others who prayed*—Have you guessed yet that I have a passion for gaining inspiration from the biographies of others? I have several volumes on the life of Susannah Wesley...and that's just the beginning of my bookcase full of publications that chronicle the journeys God's servants, a faithful cloud of witnesses, have taken with Him down through the centuries. Each person I journey alongside becomes a friend, a teacher, a model, and a spiritual coach.

But let me encourage you to take your reading a step further. Journal what you are learning! Copy out the most moving passages and quotes from these books. Keep a record of your time spent investigating that person's life. And if you can, type or input all that you want to keep from that book. Yes, I mark in my books, but I can't always carry the books with me. However, I can carry my journal or five to ten typed pages anywhere...and then sit back and be re-instructed, re-challenged, and re-inspired.

(And here's another P.S.: Copy and keep the quotes on prayer that you like whenever you run across them. You can do this for any topic that contributes to your spiritual growth ...but especially do it for prayer!)

8. *Reflect on and study the prayers of the Bible*—I've been sharing a lot of my "favorites" throughout this book—favorite quotes, stories, scriptures, books and authors, heroes of the faith, and prayer practices. But as I think about this particular means of improving your prayer-life, I have two more favorites.

First, I have a favorite book entitled *All the Prayers of the Bible*, by Herbert Lockyer.[6] This scholar and devotional writer dissects and beautifully teaches through each prayer in the Bible from Genesis to Revelation. For several years this volume has been my companion as I read through my Bible. It is definitely a book I recommend for your personal prayer library.

And second is the prayer of Mary's "soul." This prayer from the heart of our Lord's mother, found in Luke 1, verses 46-55, and referred to as "Mary's Magnificat," is worthy of its own book. Like the "Lord's Prayer" prayed by Jesus, you and I can learn much about prayer by reading and analyzing this worship prayer of Mary. One thing that is noticeable is that Mary had obviously studied and memorized parts of the prayer of another woman in the Bible. Mary's words echo and reflect a knowledge of "Hannah's prayer" from the Old Testament (1 Samuel 2:1-10).

Very briefly, Mary shows us through her inspired prayer in Luke much that would improve and enhance our own prayers. She...

- ❧ verbalized her personal joy in the Lord's work in her life (verses 46-48),

- ❧ exalted the person of God and His work "from generation to generation" (verses 49-50),

- ❧ praised God for His dealings with mankind through the sending of His Son (verses 51-53), and

- ❧ pointed to God's mercy in fulfilling the covenant promise He made to "His servant Israel" (verses 54-55).

9. *Follow through with your resolve: No decision made without prayer*—Your first decision each day must be to pray. This choice will provide you with the time and opportunity to follow through with your resolve that *no decision will be made without prayer*. As you pray over your decisions, God will lead you to find and fulfill His will for your time, your day, and your life. This, in turn, will be reflected when you say *no* to secondary things and make the decisions that allow you the time and grace to be a woman of prayer, a woman after God's own heart, a woman who answers God's call to pray, and a woman who makes her desire to pray a reality.

Beloved, being and becoming this wonderful woman takes time, including time spent in prayer, not to mention God's great grace! But amazingly, once that time is spent making decisions in prayer, then your time is better managed, spent, and saved as a result of walking in God's will. So never forget, *No decision made without prayer!* Get into the habit of praying and discovering God's direction for your precious time and life. You will be a different—and better!—person.

10. *Feed your heart and mind with God's Word*—The Bible is the major stimulus for our prayer-life. Through it God speaks to us. He fills our hearts and minds with spiritual truths. And He gives us His Spirit to help us understand and "know the things that have been freely given to us by God" (1 Corinthians 2:12). We then respond to His overtures to us through our prayers. The more we respond to His overtures to us as we read His Word, the more we are inspired to pray. Prayer is a spiritual work. And no other book or stimulus can inspire the spiritual work of prayer like the spiritual power that is contained in the Bible.

Think about it. Practically speaking, *nothing going in, equals nothing going out.* When we don't read God's Word and expose ourselves to its purity and power, we usually don't think about God and, therefore, we usually don't pray.

Also, *trivia going in, equals trivia going out.* When you hear a person talk trivia (about the latest TV talk show, movie news, gossip), you know what they are feeding on. (And the same goes for "trash"! *Trash going in, equals trash going out!*)

But *God's Word going in, equals God's Word going out.* In the case of Mary and her "Magnificat," something was—and had been—going in...for years! And that something was God's law and the knowledge of His dealings with His people. Mary's heart and soul were saturated with God's Word. How do we know this? Because, beloved, it leaked out of her lips! Because her worship prayer contains about 15 discernible references to Old Testament passages of Scripture.

Because she had obviously memorized and meditated on Hannah's prayer. In other words, her heart and soul were filled-to-overflowing with God's holy Word. And overflow it did! Her praise and prayer came gushing forth as she "magnified" the God she loved and knew so well through His Word.

Oh, to *pray* like Mary! And oh, to *be* like Mary!

Checklist for Prayer

✓ *Learn*...to leave things undone—Dirty dishes on the breakfast table? Grimy pots and pans in the sink? It sounds terrible, doesn't it? Especially when we are so careful to read so many books about good house-keeping skills and enroll in classes to learn how to keep things tidy.

But our Number One priority is God and time with God. Therefore, all things related to nurturing our relationship with Him should be the Number One thing on our to-do list. So I learned that as soon as my husband was off to work and my girls were off to school, the first thing I had to do was pray. It was the only way I could ensure that the most important thing—time in God's Word and prayer—got done first! *Then* came the housework.

And it was a struggle! Devotional writer Oswald Chambers understood this well. He writes, "We can hinder the time that should be spent with God by remembering we have other things to do. I haven't time. Of course you have not time! Take time! Strangle some other interest and make time to realize that the center of power in your life is the Lord Jesus Christ."[7]

Ask yourself the question, What do I do each day that I think is more important than spending time with God in prayer? Then remember, "Prayer does not fit us for the greater work; prayer *is* the greater work"![8] And so we learn to leave things undone... and pray!

✓ *Learn*...to switch disciplines—In many seminars and conferences, I advise women to take the discipline that is already firmly in place in their lives and then add the new discipline of prayer they are trying to nurture...*ahead of* the other, to switch the disciplines.

Here's how it works. If you already have the discipline of reading or studying your Bible in place, that discipline is already a part of your life. It's set in motion in your life. It's a habit. Now, what you need to do is put prayer *ahead of* your other discipline. Put prayer, the discipline you're desiring to nurture and desiring to add and cultivate as a new habit, *in front of* the discipline that's already in place. For example, you already know you'll read your Bible. You already know how to do that. It's already a habit. Now you want to pray first...*and then* read your Bible. You want to switch the disciplines.

Or for the woman who is already disciplined to immediately tidy everything up, pick up the whole house, wash the dishes, get the kitchen sink cleaned, and the dishwasher going, the discipline of "tidiness" is already in place...but she never gets around to praying. All she has to do is switch these two desirable habits and pray first...then tidy to her heart's content! Success is certain because she already knows that she'll tidy up the house, run the dishwasher, clean the counter and the kitchen, and now she knows she'll pray, too!

So you are to simply put the discipline that's already in place *second* in order, so you can develop the habit and learn the discipline of prayer. It takes some doing—and some discipline—but you can learn to leave other things undone until you take care of one of the most important things in your life— answering God's call to prayer.

✓ *Learn...* to combine disciplines—Jim and I were invited to an annual pastors conference this past week. When it was time for me to speak to the wives who attended the convention, I spoke to them on the subject of this book—prayer. Later, at lunch, a woman who was serving at the conference, a woman who was a two-month-old "baby Christian," came to tell me when her time of prayer was. Sandy was going through physical therapy for an injury and had to ride an exercycle for 15 minutes a day at her therapist's treatment center as a part of her cure. She said she had decided to designate that 15 minutes as her prayer time! Here was a baby Christian who had already gone to work on developing the habit of prayer...and had learned to combine her disciplines!

So what other discipline could you combine with prayer? I know for three decades I've combined walking every day with memorizing Scripture. Now in the state of Washington, where there is less opportunity to walk outside, I walk on a treadmill...and you guessed it, memorize Scripture.

I've been a longtime believer in combining something physical with something spiritual. Of course, you'll want to do your laboring in prayer in private, but with a handful of 3" x 5" cards or a small notebook you can walk, run, exercycle, or treadmill...and pray! (I even know a woman who swims her laps with her prayer cards in hand...in zip-lock bags to keep them dry!)

Answering God's Call to You

Oh, dear! Our chapter is going long! But we are bringing our thoughts to a close on a most important topic—that of developing the habit of prayer.

But please, oh please, as we conclude this practical prayer-improvement section, do these two things to improve your personal prayer-life:

> Do what you must to ensure that you pray daily, regularly, habitually, and

> Do remember that prayer is not about you (or me). As you know full well, it is about God, and about your relationship with God, and about your walk with God, and about your being a woman after God's own heart.

So pray, dear heart! Answer God's call to prayer. Do whatever it takes to make your desire to pray a reality. Do whatever you must to develop the habit of prayer. And do remember, with every step along the path of your personal prayer journey, that all "prayer crowns God with the honor and glory due to His name."[9]

Dear woman of prayer, you can have no higher calling than this!

Lord,
Awaken in us the realization
That we need to call on You continually....
Teach us to have hearts that pray.
Teach us to keep ourselves focused on You.
To set up an altar in our hearts,
Where our soul might call out to
You continually. Amen.[1]

—TERRY GLASPEY

24

When You Are Anywhere and at Any Time...Pray!

*W*e did it! We made it to the end of our book about a woman's call to prayer and about our mutual desire to answer His call. As we stand here together, side by side, I am praying for *you,* dear journeying friend, and for the many things I hope were communicated to your heart.

First and foremost, my prayer was to emphasize what is *biblical* throughout this book. I wanted us to see, in part, what the Bible teaches about prayer. I pray you now have a better understanding and more insights into prayer (although, as we learned, prayer "is beyond our limited human understanding" and "is a topic too deep for the human intellect"[2]).

And definitely I prayed as I shared the *practical* elements concerning prayer. I am a nuts-and-bolts-type person. I love studying the Bible—it tells me *what* it is I am to do. But I also want to know *how* to put the *what* into practice...immediately. How to do what it is I am learning in the Bible. That's why I included the "Checklist for Prayer" after each body of teaching. And that's also why I included the reproducible "Prayer Calendar" at the back of the book. (Have you been using it all along the way? If so, I'm sure you can see progress as you've moved forward on your journey into prayer!)

Then I prayed that what I wrote would be *beneficial*. My constant prayer has been that your prayer-life will be enhanced, strengthened, sweetened, and bettered. For oh, what glory and honor such a life of prayer will bring to our God!

And all the way through I trust the undercurrent of my prayers was evident as I sought to communicate that prayer is not to be *mechanical*. My greatest fear is that in my efforts to share what the Bible teaches about prayer—the kinds of prayer, the commands to pray, and some ways to pray—you may have been discouraged from perceiving the simplicity of prayer. In no way do I want you to think that following a formula + jumping through a series of hoops = prayer!

Prayer is to be *natural!* True, prayer is hard work, a spiritual discipline. It must, like anything of value, be tended, cultivated, and cared for. But *prayer should be natural*. It should flow naturally from your heart. God has built into our hearts and souls a desire to pray, to communicate with Him, to talk to and seek fellowship with Him as our Father. When we are afraid, we "talk it over" with our Protector. When we are hurting, we "talk it over" with our Comforter. When we have been mistreated or wrongfully accused, we "talk it over" with our Advocate. When we have a need, we "talk it over" with our Provider. Indeed, we have much to "talk over" with our God!

So, as we close this volume about developing a more meaningful prayer-life, I want to leave you with these *simple* thoughts: You can—and are to—pray anywhere, at any time, and at all times! How's that for simplicity? God has made it possible for you to be successful in your desire to pray. You can...

> ...pray always (Ephesians 6:18), and

> ...pray without ceasing (1 Thessalonians 5:17).

You Can Pray Anywhere!

I love this sentiment: "The man who does all his praying on his knees does not pray enough."[3] That's true, because you and I can pray anywhere! Neither posture nor place is to limit our praying.

It's amazing that we can be attending a business or school meeting, disciplining a child, listening to a friend or husband talk to us in person or on the phone, exercising, driving on a packed, bumper-to-bumper freeway...well, you name it, and whatever it is we are doing, we can pray at the same time. We can even pray while we are speaking. In fact, we can pray the whole time we are speaking! (I know, because I do this during every seminar or message I give!)

And not only do we not miss anything that is going on or what is being said, but the very act of praying makes us more wise, sympathetic, discerning, godly, and spiritually alert. We don't miss a thing! In fact, everything we are doing is bettered by the act of prayer.

Even in sadness or when we are distraught, we can continue our work and function in a righteous way and a gracious manner because we are praying. As an early church clergyman noted, "Certain thoughts are prayers. There are moments when, whatever be the attitude of the body, the soul is on its knees."[4]

You Can Pray at Any Time!

How busy are you? I think I can guess. You're so busy you don't have time to think about how to answer this question! But you and I can thank God that because of His omnipresent nature, and because of the indwelling of the Holy Spirit in your life, you can reach out and touch God at any time through your prayers.

Here's a look at another woman who was busy. Although she was in a station of life that probably differs from yours, her attitude—and practices—should apply to your life today.

How one woman prayed without ceasing—It seems that a number of ministers were assembled for the discussion of difficult questions; and, among others, it was asked, how the command to "pray without ceasing" could be complied with.

Various suppositions were started; and at length, one of the number was appointed to write an essay upon it, to be read at the next meeting; which being overheard by a female servant, she exclaimed, "What! A whole month waiting to tell the meaning of that text? It is one of the easiest and best texts in the Bible."

"Well, well!" said an old minister. "Mary, what can you say about it? Let us know how you understand it. Can you pray all the time?"

"Oh, yes, sir!"

"What! When you have so many things to do?"

"Why, sir, the more I have to do, the more I can pray."

"Indeed! Well, Mary, do let us know how it is; for most people think otherwise."

"Well, sir," said the girl,

> "when I first open my eyes in the morning, I pray, 'Lord, open the eyes of my understanding;' and
> while I am dressing, I pray that I may be clothed with the robe of righteousness; and,
> when I have washed me, I ask for the washing of regeneration; and,
> as I begin to work, I pray that I may have strength equal to my day;
> when I begin to kindle up the fire, I pray that God's work may revive in my soul; and,
> as I sweep out the house, I pray that my heart may be cleansed from all its impurities; and,
> while preparing and partaking of breakfast, I desire to be fed with the hidden manna and the sincere milk of the word; and,
> as I am busy with the little children, I look up to God as my Father, and pray for the spirit of adoption, that I may be his child: and so on all day.
> Every thing I do furnishes me with a thought for prayer."

Needless to say, after Mary's little "exposition" on the theology of prayer, the essay was not considered necessary![5]

It's true that you and I can answer God's call to pray from anywhere and at any time. And it's true, as sweet Mary put it, that the more a busy woman has to do, the more she can pray! That is...if our hearts are tuned upward! That is...if we are even thinking about God!

From my own experience, I've noticed that the heart that prays *is* the heart that is tuned upward. The heart that prays *is* the heart that is thinking about God, that is relating everything that happens every minute throughout the day to God. It is when I am in the habit of praying each day that, lo and behold, miracle of miracles, that habit extends itself to praying all the time...everywhere...for all things...for everything!

You Can Pray All the Time!

You can pray anywhere, and you can pray any time. But you also need to be praying *all* the time! Do you remember God's two commands shared earlier in this chapter? *Pray always* (Ephesians 6:18), and *pray without ceasing* (1 Thessalonians 5:17). In other words, you are to be praying all the time, to make your every breath a prayer. As my former pastor loved to say, prayer is "spiritual breathing." You take a breath in...and a prayer goes out!

I would have to say that during the past four months, while I've been immersed in researching and writing this book about prayer and the practice of prayer, that the main impact on my life has been being conscious of praying always. Actually, prayer has become an unconscious act. It seems like, wherever I go, I am lifting up the people around me or the event I'm involved in to the Lord through prayer.

For instance, one morning while I was driving somewhere, there was a terrible accident on one of the freeways. The newscasters were talking so coldly as they reported that it was a fatal accident. It was kind of like, "Well, as soon as someone gets the bodies out of there, and the wreckage cleared away, traffic can flow smoothly again."

And you know, I just started praying about the soul of the person who had died. Was that person a believer? I also thought, *That person has family members somewhere!* and I began praying for the relatives. I just started praying that somehow, in some way, God would receive glory and honor through a fatal traffic accident and a jammed freeway filled with frustrated people!

Dear praying heart, everywhere you go, if you think of a person, pray. If you see a person (a clerk, a neighbor, a homeless man or woman, a young mom pushing a double stroller, a soldier being interviewed on the news), pray. If you know about something that's going on in a person's life, pray. Always be "praying always"! One thought-provoking question I read asked, "Are you focusing on a person's faults, or are you lifting that person before the Father?" Again, be praying always...

...like these people did:

Mary Slessor—I am greatly challenged by a diary entry in Mary Slessor's journal. She was a nineteenth-century Scottish missionary to Africa who wrote, "My life is one long daily, hourly record of answered prayer. For physical health, for mental overstrain, for guidance given marvelously, for errors and dangers averted, for enmity to the gospel subdued, for food provided at the exact hour needed, for everything that goes to make up life and my poor service to my Savior."[6]

One long daily, hourly prayer! Yes!

John Fletcher—It was the custom of John Fletcher of Madeley, England, never to meet a Christian without saying, "Friend, do I meet you praying?" This unusual salutation reminded the person that his life should be an unbroken expression of prayer and fellowship with God.[7]

An unbroken expression of prayer and fellowship with God! Yes!

Stonewall Jackson—Ian Bounds wrote describing Stonewall Jackson as a man of prayer. Jackson said, "I have so fixed the habit of prayer in my mind that I never raise a glass of water to my lips without asking God's blessing, never seal a letter without putting a word of prayer under that seal, never take a letter to the post without a brief sending of my thoughts heavenward. Never change my classes in the lecture room without a minute's petition for the cadets who go out and in those doorways."[8]

"I have so fixed the habit of prayer in my mind...." Yes!

The message is clear. We are to take every opportunity, during whatever is happening, and through every event of daily life, to pray...all the time. And we can do it, no matter what is transpiring, because...

> Prayer is the soul's sincere desire,
> Uttered or unexpressed,
> The motion of a hidden fire
> That trembles in the breast.
>
> Prayer is the burden of a sigh,
> The falling of a tear,
> The upward glancing of an eye
> When none but God is near.[9]

Checklist for Prayer

✓ *Pray*—The Bible tells you to pray faithfully, fervently, always, without ceasing, continually. Pray, too, when you are in trouble, when you are disappointed by others, when you are hurting, when you are worshiping, when you are worried, when you are overwhelmed, when you are in need, and when you must make a decision. Pray! Prayer and praying is the foremost action of a woman who is serious about answering God's call to prayer.

✓ *Praise*—I have not focused specifically on praise in this book because the subject of praise could be a book in itself. (Hmmm, I wonder…?) But praise is yet another way we worship God. So during your times of prayer, lift your praise to Him who is most worthy of it! Give praise to "the glory of His grace" (Ephesians 1:6). "Praise our God, all you His servants and those who fear Him, both small and great!" (Revelation 19:5). Let your praise flow outward and upward. It will change your outlook on life!

✓ *Proceed*—How can you become a woman who answers God's call to prayer? How can you make your desire to pray a reality? In a word, *proceed*…full steam ahead! Proceed to implement what you've learned and considered about prayer in this book. Proceed in following God's formula for effective prayer. Proceed toward finding God's will through prayer. Proceed in developing the habit of prayer. And above all, proceed in your efforts to pray from your heart!

*Forgive us for thinking that
prayer is a waste of time and
help us to see that
without prayer
our work is a waste of time.*[1]

—PETER MARSHALL

Answering God's
Call to Prayer

hroughout this book I have referred to prayer as a jewel. All along the way, you and I have been examining and admiring the many splendid facets of the precious gem of our prayers. They combine to make the jewel something special indeed, something that blazes forth and lights up your life and the lives of those you pray for, live with, and encounter. And now I want to focus one final time on prayer as a gemstone and on answering God's call to prayer.

As you know, diamonds are said to be a girl's best friend! So let's use a diamond as our jewel of choice. In my lifetime, I've seen two of the world's largest, most famous diamonds, each time while traveling with my husband on one of his ministry trips.

One was the Star of Africa, the largest cut diamond in existence. It is set in the British royal scepter, which Jim and I viewed in the Tower of London. This drop-shaped stone "weighs" in at 530.2 carats! The other was the Hope Diamond, the largest deep-blue diamond in the world, which we saw in the National Museum of Natural History at the Smithsonian Institute in Washington, D.C. (We almost didn't stay to see this one because the line was so long. But the wait was well worth it!)

But, my dear journeying friend, please realize that scientists believe brilliant, priceless diamonds like these were formed underground at depths greater than 93 miles and some as deep as 420 miles beneath the earth's surface. And so it is with an even greater jewel—your prayer-life. The holy habit of prayer is formed underground, hidden from sight, "alone with the Eternal."

Why does the formation of a diamond require such recesses? Because crystallization requires pressures and temperatures that only occur at such tremendous depths. And, oh, is that ever true of your glistening prayer-life! The more pressure, the better! The more heat, the better! Such uncomfortable conditions can only make your life of prayer more dazzling. For it is the pressures of life that press us upon God, that move us to lean upon His breast...and to seek His power and might in our weaknesses.

So purpose to answer God's call to you to pray. Purpose to hide away with Him in prayer...daily. Doing so will change you. It will change your relationships. And it will change your life. Diamonds are the hardest substance on the earth. And you, dear one, will resemble a diamond when you gather up the conditions and concerns of your life and "take it to the Lord in prayer." You will become, in a good sense, hard, tough, solid, powerful, confident, full-of-faith.

So, dear one, don't cave in under pressure! Don't give in to life's troubles! Don't disintegrate into a puddle of tears and depression! Instead take Jesus' advice to heart. He said you "always ought to pray and not lose heart" (Luke 18:1). So answer His call to prayer! Make it your lifestyle!

In His everlasting love,

Elizabeth George

Suggested Books of Prayers

The Harper Collins Book of Prayers—A Treasury of Prayers Through the Ages, compiled by Robert Van de Weyer. Edison, NJ: Castle Books, 1997.

The One Year® Book of Personal Prayer. Wheaton, IL: Tyndale House Publishers, Inc., 1991.

The Prayers of Susanna Wesley, edited and arranged by W.L. Doughty, Clarion Classics. Grand Rapids, MI: Zondervan Publishing House, 1984.

The Valley of Vision—A Collection of Puritan Prayers and Devotions, edited by Arthur Bennett. Carlisle, PA: The Banner of Truth Trust, 1999.

Notes

An Invitation to...Become a Woman of Prayer

1. J.D. Douglas, *The New Bible Dictionary* (Grand Rapids, MI: Wm. B. Eerdmans Publishing Co., 1978), p. 1019.

Chapter 1—Beginning the Journey into Prayer

1. A.A. Milne, "Vespers," from *When We Were Very Young* (New York: E.P. Dutton and Co. and Methuen Children's Books Ltd., date unknown).

2. William Law, source unknown.

Chapter 2—Ten Reasons Women Don't Pray—Part 1

1. C.E. Cowman, as quoted in Eleanor Doan, *Speaker's Sourcebook* (Grand Rapids, MI: Zondervan Publishing Company, 1988), p. 192.

2. From the hymn "Turn Your Eyes upon Jesus," by Helen M. Lemmel.

Chapter 4—Ten Reasons Women Don't Pray—Part 3

1. Psalter quoted in D.L. Moody, *Notes from My Bible and Thoughts from My Library* (Grand Rapids, MI: Baker Book House, 1979), p. 184.

2. Leonard Ravenhill, source unknown.

3. Paul S. Rees, source unknown.

4. Eleanor Doan, *Speaker's Sourcebook* (Grand Rapids, MI: Zondervan Publishing Company, 1988), p. 197.

Chapter 5—When You Are in Trouble...Pray!

1. Terry W. Glaspey, *Pathway to the Heart of God* (Eugene, OR: Harvest House Publishers, 1998), p. 13.

Chapter 6—When You Are Disappointed by Others...Pray!

1. Herbert Lockyer, *All the Prayers of the Bible* (Grand Rapids, MI: Zondervan Publishing House, 1973), p. 64.

2. Ibid., p. 37.

3. Romans 3:23; 1 Corinthians 10:12; 1 John 1:8.

Chapter 7—When You Are Hurting...Pray!

1. O. Hallesby, quoted in Terry W. Glaspey, *Pathway to the Heart of God* (Eugene, OR: Harvest House Publishers, 1998), p. 119.

2. Derek Kidner, *Psalms 1–72, An Introduction and Commentary on Books I and II of the Psalms* (Downers Grove, IL: InterVarsity Press, 1978), p. 199.

3. D.L. Moody, *Notes from My Bible and Thoughts from My Library*, quoting Cuyler (Grand Rapids, MI: Baker Book House, 1979), p. 93.

4. Adapted from Charles Caldwell Ryrie, *The Ryrie Study Bible* (Chicago: Moody Press, 1978), p. 848.

Chapter 8—When You Are Worshiping...Pray!

1. J.D. Douglas, gen. ed., *The New Bible Dictionary* (Grand Rapids, MI: Wm. B. Eerdmans Publishing Co., 1978), pp. 561, 1340.

2. John MacArthur, *The MacArthur Study Bible* (Nashville: Word Bibles, 1996), p. 867.

3. Ibid., p. 1509.

4. Walter B. Knight, *Knight's Master Book of New Illustrations* (Grand Rapids, MI: Wm. B. Eerdmans, 1956/1979), p. 491.

5. Eleanor Doan, *Speaker's Sourcebook* (Grand Rapids, MI: Zondervan Publishing House, 1988), p. 192.

Chapter 9—When You Are Worried...Pray!

1. Author unknown, taken from Albert M. Well Jr., *Inspiring Quotations* (Nashville: Thomas Nelson Publishers, 1988), p. 220.

2. William Hendriksen, *New Testament Commentary—Philippians* (Grand Rapids, MI: Baker Books, 2002), p. 194.

3. Curtis Vaughan, *The Word—The Bible from 26 Translations* (Gulfport, MS: Mathis Publishers, Inc., 1991), p. 2391.

4. See Elizabeth George, *Powerful Promises™ for Every Woman—12 Life-Changing Truths from Psalm 23* and *God Loves His Precious Children* (Eugene, OR: Harvest House Publishers, 2000 and 2004).

5. M.R. DeHaan and Henry G. Bosch, *Bread for Each Day* (Grand Rapids, MI: Zondervan Publshing House, 1980), December 11.

6. Paul J. Meyer and John C. Maxwell, *Unlocking Your Legacy* (Chicago: Moody Publishers, 2002). Used by permission.

Chapter 10—When You Are Overwhelmed...Pray!

1. Fritz Rienecker, *A Linguistic Key to the Greek New Testament—Volume 2* (Grand Rapids, MI: Zondervan Publishing House, 1981), p. 21.

2. Herbert Lockyer, *All the Prayers of the Bible* (Grand Rapids, MI: Zondervan Publishing House, 1973), p. 239.

3. *Life Application Bible Commentary—Romans* (Wheaton, IL: Tyndale House Publishers, Inc., 1992), p. 164.

4. Ibid., p. 164.

Chapter 12—When You Must Make a Decision...Pray for Faith!

1. John F. MacArthur, audiotapes #1833 and #1834, entitled "The Limits of Our Liberty, Part 1 and 2" [1 Corinthians 8:1-13] (Grace to You, P.O Box 4000, Panorama City, CA 91412). © 1975 by John MacArthur.

2. Eleanor Doan, *Speaker's Sourcebook*, quoting Edward Payton (Grand Rapids, MI: Zondervan Publishing House, 1988), p. 192.

Chapter 13—When You Must Make a Decision...Pray for Wisdom!—Part 1

1. Charles R. Swindoll, *The Tale of the Tardy Oxcart* (Nashville: W Publishing Group, 1998), p. 613.

Chapter 14—When You Must Make a Decision...Pray for Wisdom!—Part 2

1. Acts 9:6; Luke 22:42.
2. Psalm 19:14; Galatians 5:16,22-23; Ephesians 4:1.
3. Psalm 139:23-24; 5:3; James 5:16.
4. To review, you now have James 1:5; 4:17; Proverbs 3:5-6.

Chapter 15—When You Must Make a Decision...Pray for Order!

1. Derek Kidner, *The Proverbs* (Downers Grove, IL: InterVarsity Press, 1973), p. 177.
2. Charles R. Swindoll, *The Tale of the Tardy Oxcart*, quoting Wayne Martindale, *The Quotable Lewis* (Nashville: Word Publishing, 1998), p. 468.
3. W.L. Doughty, ed., *The Prayers of Susanna Wesley* (Grand Rapids, MI: Zondervan Publishing House, 1984), p. 46.
4. Elizabeth George, *Life Management for Busy Women* (Eugene, OR: Harvest House Publishers, 2002), p. 239.

Chapter 16—When You Must Make a Decision...Pray for Understanding!

1. Author unknown, quoted in Eleanor Doan, *Speaker's Sourcebook,* (Grand Rapids, MI: Zondervan Publishing House, 1988), p. 283.
2. Roy B. Zuck, *The Speaker's Quote Book*, quoting Charles Neilsen (Grand Rapids, MI: Kregel Publications, 1997), p. 409.
3. Ibid., p. 110.
4. Ibid., pp. 110-11.

Chapter 17—The Time of Prayer

1. Andrew Murray, quoted in Eleanor Doan, *Speaker's Sourcebook* (Grand Rapids, MI: Zondervan Publishing House, 1988), p. 283.
2. Sherwood Eliot Wirt and Kersten Beckstrom, *Topical Encyclopedia of Living Quotations*, quoting Paul S. Rees (Minneapolis: Bethany House Publishers, 1982), p. 181.
3. William Law, as quoted in Terry W. Glaspey, *Pathway to the Heart of God* (Eugene, OR: Harvest House Publishers, 1998), p. 152.
4. "The Difference Prayer Makes," author unknown, in Eleanor Doan, *Speaker's Sourcebook* (Grand Rapids, MI: Zondervan Publishing House, 1988), p. 198. Note: Internet source credits Grace L. Naessens for this poem.

Chapter 18—The Times of Prayer

1. Stanley High, *Billy Graham* (New York: McGraw Hill, 1956), p. 71.

2. Linda Raney Wright, *Raising Children* (Wheaton, IL: Tyndale House Publishers, Inc., 1975), p. 50.

3. S.D. Gordon, *Quiet Talks on Prayer* (Grand Rapids, MI: Fleming H. Revell, 1980), p. 191.

4. Ibid., p. 119.

5. Corrie ten Boom, *A Life of Prayer.*

6. Edith Schaeffer, *The Tapestry* (Waco, TX: Word Books, 1981), p. 615.

Chapter 19—The Place of Prayer

1. Ruth Bell Graham, "Especially for You," *Decision,* vol. 43, no. 9, September 2002, p. 42.

2. S.D. Gordon, *Quiet Talks on Prayer* (Grand Rapids, MI: Fleming H. Revell, 1980), pp. 150-58.

Chapter 20—The Posture of Prayer

1. Louis H. Evans, quoted in Albert M. Well Jr., *Inspiring Quotations* (Nashville: Thomas Nelson Publishers, 1988), p. 159.

2. Herbert Lockyer, *All the Prayers of the Bible* (Grand Rapids, MI: Zondervan Publishing House, 1973), p. 265.

3. Sandra Goodwin, "Traveling on My Knees," as cited in Paul Lee Tan, *Encyclopedia of 7700 Illustrations* (Winona Lake, IN: BMH Books, 1979), p. 1038.

4. Sam Walter Foss (1858–1911), "The Prayer of Cyrus Brown."

Chapter 21—The Voice of Prayer

1. Source unknown.

2. *Life Application Bible*, New Living Translation (Wheaton, IL: Tyndale House Publishers, 1996), p. 860.

3. Charles Caldwell Ryrie, *The Ryrie Study Bible* (Chicago: Moody Press, 1978), p. 841.

4. *Life Application Bible*, New Living Translation, p. 941.

5. Origen, early church father (c. 185–254 A.D.), as quoted in Terry W. Glaspey, *Pathway to the Heart of God,* (Eugene, OR: Harvest House Publishers, 1998) pp. 160-61.

Chapter 22—Ten Ways to Improve Your Prayer-Life—Part 1

1. Paul Lee Tan, *Encyclopedia of 7,700 Illustrations* (Winona Lake, IN: BMH Books, 1979), p. 1038.

2. Ethel M. Baldwin and David V. Benson, *The Henrietta Mears Story and How She Did It* (Ventura, CA: Regal Books, 1980), p. 98.

3. This book has since been printed with a new title, *Face to Face, Praying the Scriptures for Intimate Worship,* by Kenneth Boa, Zondervan Corporation, 1997.

4. Arthur Bennett, ed., *The Valley of Vision, A Collection of Puritan Prayers and Devotions* (Carlisle, PA: The Banner of Truth Trust, 1999), p. 127.

Chapter 23—Ten Ways to Improve Your Prayer-Life—Part 2

1. Matthew Henry, *Matthew Henry's Commentary of the Whole Bible* (Peabody, MA: Hendrickson Publishers, Inc., 2003), p. 87.
2. Rebecca Lamar Harmon, *Susanna, Mother of the Wesleys* (Nashville: Abingdon Press, 1968), p. 67.
3. Harmon, *Susanna, Mother of the Wesleys*, author's emphases, p. 92.
4. Frank S. Mead, *12,000 Religious Quotations* (Grand Rapids, MI: Baker Book House, 2000), p. 336. Internet sources attribute this quote to Henry Ward Beecher.
5. Eleanor L. Doan, *Speaker's Sourcebook* (Grand Rapids, MI: Zondervan Publishing House, 1988), p. 191. Internet sources attribut this quote to Mahatma Gandhi.
6. Herbert Lockyer, *All the Prayers of the Bible* (Grand Rapids, MI: Zondervan Publishing House, 1973).
7. Harry Verploegh, ed., *Oswald Chambers—The Best from All His Books* (Nashville: Oliver Nelson/Thomas Nelson Publishers, 1987), p. 359.
8. Doan, *Speaker's Sourcebook*, quoting Oswald Chambers, author's emphasis, p. 192.
9. Mead, *12,000 Religious Quotations*, quoting Thomas Benton Brooks, p. 337.

Chapter 24—When You Are Anywhere and at Any Time...Pray!

1. Terry W. Glaspey, quoted in Terry Glaspey, *Pathway to the Heart of God* (Eugene, OR: Harvest House Publishers, 1998), p. 133.
2. Terry W. Glaspey, *Pathway to the Heart of God,* p. 133.
3. Eleanor L. Doan, *Speaker's Sourcebook*, (Grand Rapids, MI: Zondervan Publishing House), p. 193.
4. Frank S. Mead, *12,000 Religious Quotations*, quoting Victor Hugo (Grand Rapids, MI: Baker Book House, 2000), p. 341.
5. Elon Foster, *6000 Sermon Illustrations* (Grand Rapids, MI: Baker Book House, 1992), p. 511.
6. Vinita Hampton and Carol Plueddemann, *World Shapers: A Treasury of Quotes from Great Missionaries* (Wheaton, IL: Harold Shaw Publishers, 1991), p. 46.
7. Roy B. Zuck, *The Speaker's Quote Book*, quoting "Our Daily Bread" (Grand Rapids, MI: Kregel Publications, 1997), p. 294. (February 21, 2004).
8. Ian Bounds, source unknown.
9. Mead, *12,000 Religious Quotations*, quoting James Montgomery, *What Is Prayer?* p. 344.

Answering God's Call to Prayer

1. Peter Marshall, as quoted in Roy B. Zuck, *The Speaker's Quote Book* (Grand Rapids, MI: Kregel Publications, 1997), p. 298.

$\mathcal{P}$rayer $\mathcal{C}$alendar*

Jan.	Feb.	Mar.	Apr.	May	June
1	1	1	1	1	1
2	2	2	2	2	2
3	3	3	3	3	3
4	4	4	4	4	4
5	5	5	5	5	5
6	6	6	6	6	6
7	7	7	7	7	7
8	8	8	8	8	8
9	9	9	9	9	9
10	10	10	10	10	10
11	11	11	11	11	11
12	12	12	12	12	12
13	13	13	13	13	13
14	14	14	14	14	14
15	15	15	15	15	15
16	16	16	16	16	16
17	17	17	17	17	17
18	18	18	18	18	18
19	19	19	19	19	19
20	20	20	20	20	20
21	21	21	21	21	21
22	22	22	22	22	22
23	23	23	23	23	23
24	24	24	24	24	24
25	25	25	25	25	25
26	26	26	26	26	26
27	27	27	27	27	27
28	28	28	28	28	28
29	29	29	29	29	29
30		30	30	30	30
31		31		31	

* See pp. 19-20 in chapter 1 under "Checklist for Prayer" (third checkmark section) for instructions in using this encouraging calendar.

Date Begun_____

July	Aug.	Sept.	Oct.	Nov.	Dec.
1	1	1	1	1	1
2	2	2	2	2	2
3	3	3	3	3	3
4	4	4	4	4	4
5	5	5	5	5	5
6	6	6	6	6	6
7	7	7	7	7	7
8	8	8	8	8	8
9	9	9	9	9	9
10	10	10	10	10	10
11	11	11	11	11	11
12	12	12	12	12	12
13	13	13	13	13	13
14	14	14	14	14	14
15	15	15	15	15	15
16	16	16	16	16	16
17	17	17	17	17	17
18	18	18	18	18	18
19	19	19	19	19	19
20	20	20	20	20	20
21	21	21	21	21	21
22	22	22	22	22	22
23	23	23	23	23	23
24	24	24	24	24	24
25	25	25	25	25	25
26	26	26	26	26	26
27	27	27	27	27	27
28	28	28	28	28	28
29	29	29	29	29	29
30	30	30	30	30	30
31	31		31		31

If you've benefited from *A Woman's Call to Prayer*, you'll want the companion volume

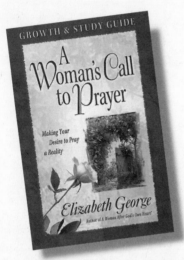

A Woman's Call to Prayer

Growth and Study Guide

This guide offers additional Scriptures, thought-provoking questions, reflective studies, and personal applications that will enrich your prayer life.

This growth and study guide is perfect for both personal and group use.

A Woman's Call to Prayer Gowth and Study Guide is available at your local Christian bookstore or can be ordered from:

Jim and Elizabeth George Ministries
P.O. Box 2879
Belfair, WA 98528
Toll-free fax/phone: 1-800-542-4611
www.elizabethgeorge.com

About the Author

Elizabeth George is a bestselling author and speaker whose passion is to teach the Bible in a way that changes women's lives. For information about Elizabeth's books or speaking ministry, to sign up for her mailings, or to share how God has used this book in your life, please write to Elizabeth at:

Jim and Elizabeth George Ministries
P.O. Box 2879
Belfair, WA 98528

Toll-free fax/phone: 1-800-542-4611
www.elizabethgeorge.com

~

Books by Elizabeth George

Beautiful in God's Eyes—The Treasures of the Proverbs 31 Woman
God's Wisdom for Every Woman's Life
Life Management for Busy Women
Loving God with All Your Mind
Powerful Promises™ for Every Woman
The Remarkable Women of the Bible
A Wife After God's Own Heart
A Woman After God's Own Heart®
A Woman After God's Own Heart® Deluxe Edition
A Woman After God's Own Heart® Prayer Journal
A Woman's Call to Prayer
A Woman's High Calling
A Woman's Walk with God
A Young Woman After God's Own Heart

Growth & Study Guides

God's Wisdom for Every Woman's Life Growth & Study Guide
Life Management for Busy Women Growth & Study Guide
Powerful Promises™ for Every Woman Growth & Study Guide
The Remarkable Women of the Bible Growth & Study Guide
A Wife After God's Own Heart Growth & Study Guide
A Woman After God's Own Heart® Growth & Study Guide
A Woman's Call to Prayer Growth & Study Guide
A Woman's High Calling Growth & Study Guide
A Woman's Walk with God Growth & Study Guide

A Woman After God's Own Heart® Bible Study Series

Walking in God's Promises—The Life of Sarah
Cultivating a Life of Character—Judges/Ruth
Becoming a Woman of Beauty & Strength—Esther
Discovering the Treasures of a Godly Woman—Proverbs 31
Nurturing a Heart of Humility—The Life of Mary
Experiencing God's Peace—Philippians
Pursuing Godliness—1 Timothy
Growing in Wisdom & Faith—James
Putting On a Gentle & Quiet Spirit—1 Peter

Books by Jim George

A Husband After God's Own Heart
A Man After God's Own Heart
God's Man of Influence

Books by Jim & Elizabeth George

Powerful Promises™ for Every Couple
Powerful Promises™ for Every Couple Growth & Study Guide
(Coming September 2004)

Children's Books

God Loves His Precious Children (co-authored with Jim George)
God's Wisdom for Little Boys (co-authored with Jim George)
God's Wisdom for Little Girls

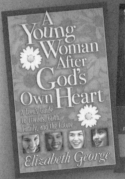
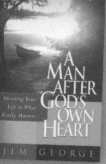

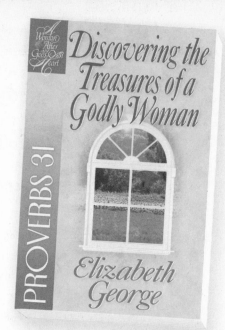

A Woman's High Calling

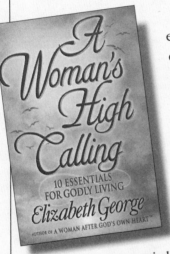

Is the cry of your heart to exchange the clutter and chaos of everyday life for a simple focus on what's really important? If so, there's no better place to look for help than the Bible. There we find the essentials God values most in a woman. *A Woman's High Calling* explores the 10 essentials for godly living as presented in Titus 2:3-5, including wisdom, purity, ministry, godly behavior, and love of home.

Start simplifying your life right now by putting these priorities into practice in all that you do...and experience the joy that comes from living in a way that pleases God and fulfills His purposes for your life.